TACTICAL QUESTIONING

TACTICAL QUESTIONING
SCENES FROM THE
BAHA MOUSA INQUIRY

Edited by
Richard Norton-Taylor

OBERON BOOKS
LONDON
WWW.OBERONBOOKS.COM

First published in 2011 by Oberon Books Ltd
521 Caledonian Road, London N7 9RH
Tel: +44 (0) 20 7607 3637 / Fax: +44 (0) 20 7607 3629
e-mail: info@oberonbooks.com
www.oberonbooks.com

A catalogue record for this book is available from the British
Library.

ISBN: 978-1-84943-031-9

Printed in Great Britain by CPI Antony Rowe, Chippenham.

The Tricycle Theatre

'The Tricycle Theatre is an inspirational example of how art with a social conscience need not require creative compromise.'
Liberty Human Rights Award, November 2010

The Tricycle Theatre has established a unique reputation for presenting plays that reflect the cultural diversity of its community, in particular by Black, Irish, Jewish, Asian and South African writers, as well as for responding to contemporary issues and events with its ground-breaking 'tribunal plays' and political work.

'The history of British drama in the past 15 years must be revised. Surely its most important development has been the Tricycle docu-dramas.'

Financial Times, 2005

In 1994 it staged the first of its tribunal plays: *Half the Picture* by Richard Norton-Taylor and John McGrath (a dramatisation of the Scott Arms to Iraq Inquiry), which was the first play ever to be performed in the Houses of Parliament. The next, marking the fiftieth anniversary of the 1946 War Crimes Tribunal, was *Nuremberg*, which was followed by *Srebrenica* – The 1996 UN Rule 61 Hearings, which later transferred to the National Theatre and the Belfast Festival. In 1999, the Tricycle's reconstruction of the Stephen Lawrence Inquiry, *The Colour of Justice*, transferred to the West End and the National Theatre. In 2003 *Justifying War – Scenes from the Hutton Inquiry* opened and *Bloody Sunday – Scenes from the Saville Inquiry* followed in 2005, which was also performed at the Abbey in Dublin, Belfast and Derry. It received an Olivier Award for Outstanding Achievement. *Called to Account* – A hearing about the indictment of Tony Blair for the crime of aggression against Iraq – was staged at the Tricycle with evidence from Richard Perle, the Chilean Ambassador to the U.N. and ex-Cabinet Minister Clare Short. All of these plays have been broadcast by the BBC on radio or television, and have together reached audiences of over 30 million people worldwide.

'With its verbatim theatre productions ... the Tricycle Theatre has consistently exposed significant fault-lines in British society and the way we are governed.'

The Daily Telegraph, 2009

In 2004, the critically-acclaimed *Guantanamo – Honor Bound to Defend Freedom*, written by Victoria Brittain and Gillian Slovo from spoken evidence, transferred from the Tricycle to the West End and New York (where Archbishop Tutu appeared in the production). In 2006 the Tricycle presented a performance of the play at the Houses of Parliament and on Washington's Capitol Hill. It has since been performed around the world and in the US through the 'Guantanamo Reading Project', which develops community productions of readings of the play in cities across America.

'The Tricycle Theatre has a matchless record in exposing injustice'

The Guardian, 2009

Notable theatre productions staged at the Tricycle have included the British premiere of *The Great White Hope* by Howard Sackler (later re-staged for the Royal Shakespeare Company), the world premiere of *Playboy of the West Indies* by Mustapha Matura, which subsequently received more than twenty productions all over the world and was televised for the BBC. West End transfers from the Tricycle also include *The Amen Corner* by James Baldwin, the Fats Waller musical *Ain't Misbehavin'* and *The Price* by Arthur Miller; and transfers to Broadway include: the South African musical *Kat and the Kings* (winner of two 1999 Olivier Awards for Best New Musical and Best Actor – awarded to the entire cast), *Stones in his Pockets* by Marie Jones, and *39 Steps* adapted by Patrick Barlow (both won Olivier awards in the West End for Best New Comedy).

In November 2006, the Tricycle was proud to win a Special

Award at the Evening Standard Theatre Awards for 'its pioneering political work'.

In 2005/6 the Tricycle pioneered a black ensemble company in three British premieres of African-American plays chronicling the black experience of the last hundred years: *Walk Hard* by Abram Hill, *Gem of the Ocean* by the late August Wilson and *Fabulation* by Lynn Nottage. The Tricycle has also premiered six of August Wilson's decalogue chronicling the African-American experience of twentieth-century plays.

2009 saw the success of a season of full-length plays by Roy Williams, Kwame Kwei-Armah & Bola Agbaje, entitled *Not Black and White*, looking at 21st-century London from a black perspective. And following the general election in 2010 the Tricycle presented *Women, Power and Politics*, a season of twelve new plays which examined both the history of women's role in politics and the complex issues surrounding contemporary women's participation and role in government.

'There is no theatre in Britain that punches so consistently above its size and weight than the Tricycle'

The Daily Telegraph, 2009

In the summer of 2009 the Tricycle also launched its seven-hour trilogy *The Great Game: Afghanistan*, which premiered plays by Richard Bean, David Edgar, David Greig, Amit Gupta, Ron Hutchinson, Stephen Jeffreys, Abi Morgan, Ben Ockrent, J.T. Rogers, Simon Stephens, Colin Teevan, and Joy Wilkinson. The production received an Olivier Award Nomination for Outstanding Achievement and was revived at the Tricycle in summer 2010, with several of the plays updated to reflect the changes in the conflict. The production completed a tour of the USA in the autumn of 2010, starting in Washington DC and travelling to Minneapolis, Minnesota; Berkeley, California and finally New York where it was met with generous praise from key policy-makers in American politics. In February 2011, the production returned to Washington to play two command performances for Pentagon staff, the military, policy-makers, aid-workers and guests.

'The Tricycle often offers the most politically audacious programming of any theatre in London'

Financial Times, 2010

Education and community activities are an integral part of the artistic output of the Tricycle: particular emphasis is placed on social exclusion.

The Tricycle's home in the London borough of Brent comprises a theatre, cinema, art gallery, café and bar, and it is open all year round.

'Britain's leading political playhouse'

The Times, 2011

An Overview of the Baha Mousa Inquiry

Thousands of British soldiers took part in the US-invasion of Iraq, ill-prepared and badly-informed. Their commanders were under the illusion, based on poor intelligence, that the overwhelming majority of Iraqis would welcome them with open arms, that much of the Iraqi army would remain in place and help maintain law and order after Saddam Hussein was toppled. If there was going to be any problem at all it would be a humanitarian one with Iraqis desperate to escape the bombing.

Lack of preparation and inadequate training of British (and US) forces, so clearly exposed at the Chilcot inquiry, paved the way to a violent insurgency. A potentially welcoming and enthusiastic population became a deeply disappointed, disillusioned, and embittered one, that quickly came to see foreign troops as occupiers not liberators.

Gerard Elias, QC, Counsel to the Baha Mousa Inquiry put it this way: 'As well as increasing disorder, looting, and the activities of insurgent groups, soldiers were required to cope with very difficult environmental conditions. The temperature in Iraq in September regularly exceeds 50 degrees centigrade. Many soldiers suffered from heat exhaustion. In addition to the conventional military function of providing armed security, British forces found themselves in a civilian policing role and responsible for running much of the city's infrastructure. Soldiers were sometimes working very, very long hours, often with little respite'.

Colonel Jorge Mendonca, commander of 1 Battalion Queen's Lancashire Regiment (1QLR), who with six of his soldiers faced a court martial, told the Inquiry: 'I cannot begin to describe what it feels like to be in 58 degrees centigrade. When we turned up in Kuwait, I think it was 45 and I felt like I had walked into an oven'.

All this may help to explain, but not excuse, the abuse of Iraqi civilians. It became clear that British soldiers had little or no idea of the legal, let alone moral, boundaries of behaviour. The case of Baha Mousa and others in Iraq led General Dannatt, the former Head of the Army, to suggest that many members of the

Armed Forces lacked moral values when they joined up. 'I think you've got to look at the proportion of people who come into the Armed Forces from chaotic backgrounds', he said recently. Respect for others, he added, was 'almost the most important' of all the values soldiers were taught. Without it, he warned, 'that's when you're into bullying or abusing Iraqi citizens'.

Yet the soldiers' commanders and even the Ministry of Defence's own senior lawyers were uncertain and divided about the law. The chain of command appeared confused. They were unaware of the ban imposed by Prime Minister Edward Heath in 1972, following an official inquiry and ruling by the European Court of Human Rights, on what became known as the 'five techniques' – wall-standing, hooding, subjection to noise, deprivation of sleep, and deprivation of food and drink.

General Sir Michael Walker, Chief of the Defence staff at the time of Baha Mousa's death, said he didn't remember being aware of the Heath ruling and had 'no inkling' detainees were hooded for long periods.

Baha Mousa was a 26-year-old hotel receptionist, whose wife had recently died of cancer, aged 22. He was arrested, along with nine other Iraqis, at the Haitham Hotel in Basra on 14 September 2003 by soldiers from 1QLR. Rifles, bayonets and suspected bomb-making equipment were found at the scene. Many Iraqis traditionally had arms to defend themselves against criminals or tribal enemies. Many more did so in the chaotic aftermath of the US-led invasion. A month earlier, an officer serving with the QLR was blown up in a marked ambulance.

Mousa, the son of an Iraqi police colonel, was held at a temporary detention centre with the other civilians for 36 hours, more than 23 hours hooded. Two days after his arrest, on 15 September 2003, Mousa died. A post-mortem examination found he had suffered asphyxiation and at least 93 injuries to his body, including fractured ribs and a broken nose.

There is evidence that army officers and MoD officials wanted to cover up the circumstances of Mousa's death. Certainly they were in no hurry to have it investigated by the Military Police. Lord Goldsmith, Attorney General at the time, expressed his concern in a letter to Geoff Hoon in March 2005. 'I have been extremely concerned at the conduct of the investigations carried out in a number of the cases which have been referred to the Army Prosecuting Authority arising out of the Iraq conflict', he told Hoon. He added: 'I have become most concerned about the quality of investigation into the death of Baha Mousa and the assaults against others detained with him in an incident which occurred on 14/15 September 2003. The matter was not referred to the [prosecuting authority] until 23 June 2004'.

Martin Hemming, the MoD's chief legal adviser, admitted the MoD failed to seek the advice of Goldsmith, who held the view that British soldiers were bound by the European Human Rights Act in places such as detention centres, which they controlled. Colonel Nicholas Mercer, the army's chief legal adviser strongly opposed to hooding, walked out of a meeting with the Red Cross in Iraq because he was told by defence officials not to speak at it.

Major General Robin Brims, commander of all British forces in southern Iraq, issued an order banning hooding in April 2003, five months before Mousa's death. He admitted his order was distributed 'patchily'. Geoff Hoon, Defence Secretary at the time, said he was unaware of that.

Ministers, including Hoon and his Armed Forces Minister, Adam Ingram, appeared not to want to know what some British troops were up to in Iraq. Mendonca, who left the army in apparent disgust at the way he had been treated, told the Inquiry he was 'wholly unaware' of the state of his regiment's detention facility in Basra.

A six-month court martial – the most expensive in British history – ended in April 2007 with six soldiers of the QLR, now the Duke of Lancaster's Regiment, cleared of abusing civilian detainees and in Mendonca's case, negligence. A seventh soldier, 36-year-old Corporal Donald Payne, admitted inhumane treatment, was jailed for a year and dismissed from the army, becoming the UK's first convicted war criminal under the International Criminal Court Act. The judge presiding over the court martial accused QLR soldiers of erecting 'a wall of silence' around the case.

That was not the end of a matter which General Sir Mike Jackson described as 'a stain on the character of the British Army', and one that would remain until it had been solved. Lawyers for the Iraqis, notably Phil Shiner, applied to the High Court for a proper independent inquiry as required by the Human Rights Act in cases where agents of the state – in this case, British soldiers – were involved in abuses.

In March 2008, the Ministry of Defence admitted breaching the human rights of the detainees held in Basra. It agreed to pay £2.83m compensation to Baha Mousa's family and the nine surviving detainees held with him. The then Defence Secretary, Des Browne, admitted 'substantive breaches' of the European Convention on Human Rights which enshrines the right to life and prohibits torture. Browne said the court martial had highlighted important questions that needed to be answered. An Inquiry was important to 'reassure the public that we are leaving no stone unturned'. The Inquiry, under Sir William Gage, a recently retired appeal court judge, began in July 2009. He was expected to publish his findings this month, June 2011. The Inquiry revealed a litany of buck-passing, irresponsibility, ignorance, and incompetence. The MoD's defence was expressed by Bob Ainsworth, Browne's successor as Defence Secretary, when he said: 'Over 120,000 British troops have served in Iraq and the conduct of the vast majority has been of the highest order'. He added: 'Although there have been instances of misconduct, only a tiny number of individuals have been shown to have fallen short of our high standards'.

Richard Norton-Taylor

Tactical Questioning: Scenes from the Baha Mousa Inquiry edited by Richard Norton-Taylor was first performed on 2nd June 2011 at The Tricycle Theatre, London.

Cast in order of appearance:
SIR WILLIAM GAGE (Chairman of the Inquiry), Alan Parnaby
GERARD ELIAS QC (Council to the Inquiry), Thomas Wheatley
DETAINEE 002, Lewis Alsamari
INTERPRETER, Rick Warden
AARON COOPER, Luke Harris
ADRIAN REDFEARN, Mark Stobbart
CRAIG RODGERS, Christopher Fox
DONALD PAYNE, Dean Ashton
MAJOR MICHAEL PEEBLES, Rick Warden
LIEUTENANT COLONEL NICHOLAS MERCER, David Michaels
THE RT. HON. ADAM INGRAM, Simon Rouse

Director, Nicolas Kent
Designer, Polly Sullivan
Lighting, Charlie Hayday
Sound & Audio Visual, Ed Borgnis
Assistant Director, Sophie Lifschutz
Production Manager, Shaz McGee
Company Manager, Lizzie Chapman
Deputy Stage Manager, Charlotte Padgham
Assistant Stage Manager, Chiara Canal
Casting Director, Marilyn Johnson
Set Construction, Russell Carr
Associate Producer, Zoe Ingenhaag

This play was commissioned with the support of The Joseph Rowntree Charitable Trust.

Any text in square brackets was inserted by the editor or company for clarity.

OPENING STATEMENT BY COUNSEL TO THE INQUIRY
13 JULY 2009

CHAIRMAN (SIR WILLIAM GAGE): Yes, Mr Elias.

ELIAS: Thank you sir. I appear as counsel to the Inquiry. The Inquiry is primarily concerned with the circumstances surrounding the death in September 2003 of Baha Mousa and the treatment of others detained with him in Basra, Iraq, by soldiers of the 1st Battalion The Queen's Lancashire Regiment. The death of any person in the custody of the state, other than by natural causes, is always a matter raising serious questions. Where the death has occurred in the custody of British forces serving abroad these matters are of clear and obvious public concern and importance which require an independent and thorough enquiry to ascertain where possible the truth of what occurred and, where appropriate, to attribute responsibility.

There is little doubt [the regiment] faced a very challenging operational environment in Iraq. As well as increasing disorder, looting, and the activities of insurgent groups, soldiers were required to cope with very difficult environmental conditions. The temperature in Iraq in September regularly exceeds 50 degrees centigrade. Many soldiers suffered from heat exhaustion. In addition to the conventional military function of providing armed security, British forces found themselves in a civilian policing role and responsible for running much of the city's infrastructure. Soldiers were sometimes working very, very long hours, often with little respite.

Early in the morning of Sunday 14 September, [1st Battalion, Queen's Lancashire Regiment] searched various hotels in Basra. 'Salerno' was the name given to that operation. The stated intention of Operation Salerno was to find 'former regime loyalists' and Iranian insurgents who were thought to be staying in hotels in Basra. Hotel Ibn Al Haitham was one of the hotels searched. Soldiers found a quantity of weapons, along with fake identity cards and other suspicious materials. Seven people, including Baha Mousa, were detained.

There can be little doubt but that the detainees, or some of them, were the victims of physical assaults. The detainees' evidence is that they were beaten more or less continually over the 48-hour period of their detention. The detainees say they were subjected to various other forms of physical and personal abuse. There is evidence that the detainees were made to endure disgusting conditions in the facility. Some soldiers say that the detainees had urinated and defecated in their own clothing and that they were effectively left in their own excrement. The detention facility was quite open. It had no doors and any soldier passing by would, it seems, be able to wander in. There was shouting, moaning and even screaming coming from the [facility] from time to time during the detention, according to some witnesses, and the Inquiry will hear scandalous accounts of an orchestrated 'choir' of victims' reactions.

Lastly and most importantly perhaps of the events that I outline now, there occurred the death of Baha Mousa in British custody. He died at around 10 o'clock in the evening, on Monday 15 September [2003]; that is to say approximately 36 hours after his arrival at [the detention facility]. A post-mortem was conducted six days later by a pathologist, Dr Ian Hill. Dr Hill found 93 separate injuries on Baha Mousa's body, including extensive bruising over his head, torso and limbs, a fractured nose and two fractured ribs. He concluded that the injuries were consistent with a systematic beating.

We now propose to play a short extract of video film. The video shows the early stages of the detention of these detainees during the daytime on the Sunday. It shows Corporal Payne using techniques of hooding and stress positions and noise. The voice that can be heard on the video is that of Corporal Payne. I would ask that that video be played at this stage.

[Video shown.]

Sir, I am moving to the approach of government, the Ministry of Defence and the army to so-called conditioning techniques from the time of internment in Northern Ireland in the early 1970s up to and including March 2003, which was, of course, the date of the invasion of Iraq. That was the decision of the Prime Minister, Edward Heath, given to the House of Commons on 2 March 1972. I am going to read [an] extract: 'The Government, having reviewed the whole matter with great care and with particular reference to any future operations, have decided that the five techniques will not be used in future as an aid to interrogation.' Nobody, so far as the Inquiry is concerned, appears to suggest that in the 30 succeeding years Parliament did authorise the use of these five techniques [wall-standing, hooding, subjection to noise, deprivation of sleep, and deprivation of food and drink] by the armed forces as an aid to interrogation. Yet, even if one considers only the video that we have just looked at, it may be thought to be entirely apparent that these detainees were being subjected to techniques which had been prohibited in 1972.

12 OCTOBER 2009

From the evidence of Witness Detainee 002 (D002 gave evidence in person on the 30th September 2009, but the hearing was discontinued when the witness broke down).

CHAIRMAN: Good morning, ladies and gentlemen. I am just going to say a word to Mr D002.

Good morning Mr D002. If you can hear me, I am going to explain – please sit down – that your voice I don't think can be heard in this room, but we shall be hearing the translation in this room. The next thing I want to explain to you – I would be grateful if you respond 'yes' – is that you understand that you are under oath. Translator, did he say 'yes'?

INTERPRETER: I couldn't hear him, sir.

CHAIRMAN: Mr D002, could you speak up please? The interpreters are having difficulty in hearing you.

D002: Yes.

CHAIRMAN: I think we all heard that. All right. You are still under oath.

ELIAS: Mr D002, I am going to ask you some questions now. Can you hear and see me?

D002:Yes

ELIAS: I want to ask you about your treatment when you were at that detention centre by putting to you a number of questions. First of all, when you were in the detention centre, was your head hooded with something?

D002: Yes, it was.

ELIAS: Through the period of your detention, were you hooded with one hood or ever more than one hood?

D002: Three hoods.

ELIAS: At what stage do you say the three hoods were put on, from the beginning or some later stage?

D002: At all stages.

ELIAS: After your arrival at the detention centre, how soon or how long after were the hoods put on your head?

D002: After about fifteen minutes.

ELIAS: Between that time [on] the Sunday when the hoods were put on your head and the Tuesday morning when you left the detention centre, were the hoods taken off your head for any reason that you can remember?

D002: Yes.

ELIAS: For what reason?

D002: When they brought us water and food.

ELIAS: Were you ever examined by a medic or doctor or a soldier who might have been a medic?

D002: No.

ELIAS: In that detention room, Mr D002, were you made – instructed – to try to hold any particular body position?

D002: Yes.

ELIAS: Can you describe that or demonstrate it so that we can see it on the screen?

D002: Many, many – I need to remember. Many positions, hands stretched forward like this *(Indicating.)* and also our legs bent while we were leaning on the wall.

ELIAS: I understand. Can you remember whether you were able to drink whenever you wanted to?

D002: But it was never enough. The water was never enough.

ELIAS: Over that period from the Sunday to the Tuesday, apart from the bags over your head and the positions that you were made to hold, can you tell us what was done to you?

D002: They hit me on the back and they hit me with metal they got off the pane of the window.

ELIAS: Apart from the metal from the window –

INTERPRETER: I'm sorry, there are lots of noises through my ear. I can't hear distinctly. Sorry about that.

CHAIRMAN: I am afraid that is coming through to all of us.

ELIAS: Mr D002, let me ask the question again. Are you able to hear me? Apart from the metal on your back, were you hit or struck with anything else?

D002: They hit me with a pipe.

ELIAS: Apart from the pipe, do you remember being hit or struck with anything else?

D002: The metal piece as well, in addition to punching and kicking.

ELIAS: I don't want you to guess, D002, but have you any idea, over the period of time that we are talking about, how many soldiers were involved in ill-treating or assaulting you?

D002: Many soldiers.

ELIAS: The blows that were struck to you, were they aimed at any particular part of your head or body?

D002: On the kidney area, on my chest as well.

ELIAS: Could you tell the chairman of the Inquiry, Mr D002, what was the effect on you of having these hoods on your head as you have described for hour after hour?

D002: They affected my breathing.

ELIAS: Do you mean you found it difficult to breathe?

D002: Yes.

ELIAS: You speak in your statement to the Inquiry – paragraph 53 – of there coming a time when you collapsed. Do you remember that?

D002: That's correct.

ELIAS: What caused you to collapse, do you know?

D002: The severity of the beating, I lost control of myself.

ELIAS: Can you remember what, if anything, happened to you when you collapsed?

D002: I remember when I fell, collapsed, a soldier came, and lifted me up while shouting at me in English and I don't know any English. Is this the justice? Is this the humanity? Where are the human rights?

ELIAS: So the –

D002: Britain is a great country. Where are the human rights? How come we have this treatment?

ELIAS: Mr D002 –

D002: How come? How? What a treatment? Why this treatment? You liberated us from Saddam Hussein and you did this to us. Why?

ELIAS: Mr D002 –

D002: Not only one soldier you can't single out, you know all the soldiers. Even those who treated us badly, you know them very well.

CHAIRMAN: Can we just pause a moment?

D002: Where is the justice? Where are the rights?

CHAIRMAN: I think we had better break off to find out whether he is able to continue.
We are going to break off, Mr D002.

AARON COOPER, 10 NOVEMBER 2009

CHAIRMAN: Good morning ladies and gentlemen, before we start our first witness, there is one thing I want to say about tomorrow. As I am sure nearly all of you know, or have remembered, tomorrow is Armistice Day. What I propose to do tomorrow is to take our ten-minute break between five to 11 and five past 11, so that during that time each person can observe Armistice Day in any way they chose. Thank you very much.

ELIAS: Thank you sir, then I call Aaron Paul Cooper, please.

CHAIRMAN: Please stand up, Mr Cooper. I am going to ask you if you want to take the oath. I think you want to affirm, is that right?

COOPER: Yes.
AARON PAUL ANTHONY COOPER (affirmed)

CHAIRMAN: If you would be kind enough to sit down.

COOPER: Thank you, Sir.

ELIAS: In the statement that you made to this Inquiry – paragraph 39, at the foot of the page you refer to your training and the 'classroom sessions' as you call them. You say this:
'The classroom sessions were all well and good, but I do not remember putting anything that we were taught in the classrooms into practice when I got to Iraq. We just followed instructions of our superiors. This is the way the army works. I trusted that what I was being told by my superiors was right, and the way things should be done.' That is how you viewed it, is it?

COOPER: Yes.

ELIAS: I want to ask you a little, please, about Captain Dai Jones and his death. He was held in very high regard, was he?

COOPER: Yes, sir.

ELIAS: He died in August [2003], as we know. You describe his death in your statement as being a 'real standout event for everyone'.

COOPER: Yes.

ELIAS: What effect did his death have on the soldiers of 1QLR?

COOPER: We was quite upset, the fact we was going out there to do a job and trying to get Basra City back to some kind of normality after the war. We were – obviously – Dai Jones was attacked while in a marked ambulance. Obviously the lads was very angry, upset.

ELIAS: You say in your statement that [your multiple] became generally more aggressive.

COOPER: Yes.

ELIAS: 'In addition, after Captain Dai Jones' death our briefings with Lieutenant Rodgers were much more serious and "down to business".' True?

COOPER: True, yes.

ELIAS: 'We left the briefings feeling much more pumped up'.

COOPER: Yes Sir.

ELIAS: Can we move on, please, to Operation Salerno. You know what I'm talking about when I refer to that operation?

COOPER: Yes, I do, yes.

ELIAS: Did you ever hear any rumour, or anything said, that indicated these detainees had anything at all to do with the death of Captain Dai Jones?

COOPER: I do remember something being mentioned, I think by Lieutenant Rodgers.

ELIAS: What did he say? I don't mean the exact words; what was the gist of what he said?

COOPER: It was possible we were going to do some hotel – a hotel raid to find bomb making equipment and weapons, and there was a possibility that it could be in connection with the death of Captain Dai Jones.

ELIAS: Later that Sunday, did you go to the TDF?

COOPER: I did, yes.

ELIAS: About how many detainees did you see in that room at that time?

COOPER: 6 or 7.

ELIAS: In what condition were they? Were they standing; were they sitting; were they free to move about?

COOPER: No, they were in stress positions, hooded, plasticuffed.

ELIAS: What was the stress position they were in?

COOPER: Arms out in front of them, backs away from the wall.

ELIAS: And crouching, as it were?

COOPER: Some may have been crouching.

ELIAS: And what were conditions inside that room like when you went in?

COOPER: Not very good.

ELIAS: Why not?

COOPER: It's a small dark room. It didn't smell too pleasant.

ELIAS: What did it smell of?

COOPER: Excrement.

ELIAS: What was happening when you went into the room?

COOPER: The detainees were being shouted at to stay in the stress positions.

ELIAS: Who was shouting at the detainees?

COOPER: Other soldiers who were in the room.

ELIAS: Apart from shouting, were they doing anything?

COOPER: Yes.

ELIAS: What?

COOPER: Physically hitting the detainees.

ELIAS: Hitting detainees in what way?

COOPER: As you would normally hit in a fight.

ELIAS: Punches?

COOPER: Yes.

ELIAS: Punches with the fist?

COOPER: Yes.

ELIAS: And where were the blows being struck?

COOPER: Various parts of the body. Mainly the head, the abdomen region.

ELIAS: Can you tell us the names of any of the multiple who did throw a punch?

COOPER: Myself, Lieutenant Rodgers, Corporal Redfearn, Private Aspinall, Private Appleby, Private Allibone.

ELIAS: In that period of time, did you see Corporal Payne punching anyone?

COOPER: Yes, I did, yes.

ELIAS: So, would this be right, Mr Cooper – and don't just take it from me because I say it – when you went into that room, almost immediately what you saw was mayhem?

COOPER: Yes.

ELIAS: Soldiers having a go at detainees right left and centre?

COOPER: Yes.

ELIAS: Had you been prepared for that?

COOPER: No.

ELIAS: Why did you join in, as you say you did?

COOPER: Obviously – as I mentioned earlier, anger, frustration in regards to Captain Dai Jones. I just – I don't know, I just did what I felt inside.

ELIAS: So you went into the room, saw what you have told us you saw, joined in. How many detainees did you strike?

COOPER: I couldn't – I couldn't tell you.

ELIAS: Give us some idea?

COOPER: Three to five.

ELIAS: Three to five. What effect did your blows have on the detainees that you struck?

COOPER: I couldn't comment.

ELIAS: You have said that Lieutenant Rodgers was there striking a blow?

COOPER: Yes.

ELIAS: Is that right? Did you see that or is that something you were told?

COOPER: No I seen that myself.

ELIAS: Through that night, were there various visitors to the TDF?

COOPER: Yes, that's correct. There was various other soldiers from 1QLR and other regiments that did come into the TDF.

ELIAS: What was the purpose of the visits of those other soldiers, as far as you could see?

COOPER: Basically to do what had previously been done to the detainees in regards to throwing punches and mimicking them, and things like that.

ELIAS: Did you strike any blows after leaving the TDF on what I have called the first occasion?

COOPER: No, I didn't, no.

ELIAS: What caused you to change your conduct in that way?

COOPER: I felt quite guilty. I felt that the way that we had set upon them was out – you know, out of order, out of control.

ELIAS: So when did your conscience strike you?

COOPER: During that evening, after I had done what I had done.

ELIAS: So what was your feeling then?

COOPER: As I said, guilt. I mean, even if they did have a connection, the way that I had set upon them myself, and the others, you know, it – it was more animalistic than, you know, anyone else.

ELIAS: It was animalistic, and it wasn't justified on any basis, was it?

COOPER: No, not at all.

ELIAS: When did you first hear of the choir?

COOPER: On the Sunday evening. Basically Corporal Payne had got the detainees around him. He would poke them in the stomach for them to make a noise, and obviously because they all made different noises, they did it to each detainee once, and then went round them, and that's obviously where he got the choir from.

ELIAS: So that each detainee would make a different sound?

COOPER: Yes.

ELIAS: What was your reaction to the choir?

COOPER: At the time I found it quite humorous.

ELIAS: Did you laugh about it?

COOPER: At that moment I did.

ELIAS: Looking back on it, do you find it funny now?

COOPER: No.

ELIAS: Why not?

COOPER: Well, if I had been in their position, I'd be quite embarrassed.

ELIAS: Whilst you were at the TDF, were you aware of detainees being taken off for Tactical Questioning?

COOPER: I was aware of one being taken away.

ELIAS: How did you become aware of that?

COOPER: It was during my guard duty. The staff sergeant came in and took one of the detainees away.

ELIAS: What I want you to do, please, to assist the Inquiry, is to tell us what you remember about the incident that involved Baha Mousa.

COOPER: We more or less arrived [back] at the TDF, and we got off the vehicles. As we were stood outside I heard a scream – well not that scream, a cry for assistance. I entered the right-hand door.

ELIAS: When you went in, what happened? What did you see going on in that room?

COOPER: I seen Corporal Payne struggling with Baha Mousa. Baha Mousa wasn't wearing his hood; his plasticuffs were off. Obviously there was a struggle between the pair of them.

ELIAS: Just pause. In what position was Baha Mousa?

COOPER: Baha Mousa was stood up and Don Payne was to the rear of Baha Mousa trying to put his knee into the back of Baha Mousa's legs, to try and get him to the ground.

ELIAS: So Corporal Payne was behind. And what happened?

COOPER: Obviously I went to assist Corporal Payne in restraining Baha Mousa. We managed to get him to the floor. From that point, I'm not too sure if I found his arms or his legs, but I have held a piece of his body, you know, to stop him from moving about, because he was wriggling everywhere. Just to try to stop him from moving, to make it easier to get the plasticuffs back on to him.

ELIAS: And he went to the ground, did he?

COOPER: Yes.

ELIAS: To his knees, or further?

COOPER: I think it will have been further, all the way down to the floor.

ELIAS: Flat, facing downwards?

COOPER: Yes.

ELIAS: What happened then?

COOPER: As I have said, I assisted in trying to restrain him so Corporal Payne could get the plasticuffs on.

ELIAS: The plasticuffs are effectively put on then, on your account, are they, twice?

COOPER: Yes, that's correct.

ELIAS: The first time he breaks out of them, but they are reapplied? So what happened when Baha Mousa broke out of his plasticuffs for the second time?

COOPER: Obviously Corporal Payne was rather annoyed. I seen Corporal Payne stand up at that point. Corporal Payne has – in other words – give him a good kicking. Punches and kicks to his body.

ELIAS: Where on his body?

COOPER: Around the ribs. Rib area.

ELIAS: Did [Baha Mousa] try to get up?

COOPER: No, he didn't seem to be struggling as much.

ELIAS: And what happened to Baha Mousa?

COOPER: Obviously, with the strength of the kicks, Baha Mousa did bang his head against the wall.

ELIAS: So his head was banged against the wall, is that what you are saying?

COOPER: Yes.

ELIAS: By a kick?

COOPER: By a kick, and also previous – after that by Payne – Payne's hands as well. Corporal Payne also banged his head against the wall with his hands, by grabbing his head.

ELIAS: Again, so there is no ambiguity about it, do you mean that he was deliberately banging the head against the wall, or that was what happened as a result of his other actions?

COOPER: No, that's correct, [Payne] was doing it on purpose.

ELIAS: For how long did this attack by Corporal Payne go on?

COOPER: No more than 30 seconds.

ELIAS: What was it that brought it to an end?

COOPER: I think after Baha Mousa had stopped moving and stopped trying to protect himself, I think – I think – Payne just – to be honest Payne just stopped, and then obviously at that point there was no movement or sound from Baha Mousa.

ELIAS: So what happened when Corporal Payne stopped that?

COOPER: Obviously we was a little bit concerned, between – from myself really. I remember checking to see if there was a pulse. I couldn't feel a pulse.

ELIAS: What were you told by Corporal Payne?

COOPER: Payne basically said: '[He] banged his head against the wall, that's all'. You know, 'that's what happened, that's what we are going to say'.

ELIAS: In other words, you are saying he was putting you up to a story?

COOPER: That's correct.

ELIAS: It happened accidentally?

COOPER: That's correct.

ELIAS: Why did you go along with it?

COOPER: Obviously you are in the British Army, you all work as a team and try to stick as a team. [Then] there was a conversation between the [multiple] and Lieutenant Rodgers. He wanted to try and protect us and himself from anybody finding out about the treatment, the way that we treated them. So his suggestion was that all the blame be put on to Corporal Payne. That's the only reason I can think of for [why] things changed so dramatically. Mr Rodgers did not want anybody to find out the way that we had treated the detainees.

ADRIAN REDFEARN, 11 NOVEMBER 2009

ELIAS: You say in your statement to this Inquiry that you were put into stress positions during your own training exercises?

REDFEARN: Yes, I was.

ELIAS: Did you understand that stress positions could be used on civilians?

REDFEARN: No one had ever told me or shown me any part of any legislation or video where they were prohibited, sir.

ELIAS: What was the difference, as you understood it, Sergeant Redfearn, between the treatment of what I might call civilian detainees and prisoners of war?

REDFEARN: In my mind at the time, sir, the civilian detainees that we detained, they were prisoners of war. That was the way we had been taught.

ELIAS: From your perspective, as you understood the position, anyone who was detained, arrested, if you like, by soldiers, would be treated in exactly the same way whatever their status was?

REDFEARN: That's my opinion, sir, yes. I am not saying they would be placed in stress positions, what I'm saying is they should all be treated the same, sir.

ELIAS: Yes.

CHAIRMAN: Sergeant Redfearn, could you speak a little more slowly.

REDFEARN: I will, Sir.

CHAIRMAN: There is a good reason for that. What you are saying is being translated into Arabic and it is extremely difficult for those who are doing that work to keep up with you if you speak fast. It is a common fault that most people speak too fast, including myself very often. If you try, please, to slow down.

REDFEARN: I will do, Sir.

ELIAS: From your training or, indeed, from anywhere else, did you have as an individual soldier any guiding beacon, if you like, as to the way in which detainees should be treated?

REDFEARN: Yes, we had a video showed to us yearly but the video we were shown, sir, was well out of date. It was to do with basically fighting the Soviets and full-on war. It was nothing to do with fighting a building insurgency in Iraq.

ELIAS: When you arrived on that Monday morning, did you go into the [temporary detention facility] building?

REDFEARN: Yes, I did, sir, yes.

ELIAS: How many detainees were in that room?

REDFEARN: From what I can remember, either eight or nine, sir.

ELIAS: And what was their position and condition?

REDFEARN: They were sat down, cross-legged, basically in an U-shape against the wall, all hooded, all plasticuffed, and obviously –

CHAIRMAN: Please, not so fast.

REDFEARN: All plasticuffed and obviously in a lot worse condition than when they were taken away, sir.

ELIAS: Why obviously in a lot worse condition?

REDFEARN: Because when we arrested them, sir, they were still fully clothed, there were no marks on their bodies, there was no blood around the face. When we went in there, sir, it was a totally different scene.

ELIAS: What was it about their clothing?

REFEARN: Some of them were ripped. I think at least one of them was missing a top. But basically they were just in a lot – lot worse condition, sir.

ELIAS: Did you say something about blood?

REDFEARN: Yes, there was at least a couple of them had visible blood marks around the chin, around the neck, which I presumed had come from the nose or mouth, sir.

ELIAS: Were they hooded at this time?

REDFEARN: Yes, they was, sir.

ELIAS: And what condition physically did they seem to be in, apart from the marks?

REDFEARN: Worse for wear, sir, a lot worse for wear.

ELIAS: What did you think had happened to these detainees?

REDFEARN: That they had been assaulted, sir.

ELIAS: They had been beaten up?

REDFEARN: Yes, sir.

ELIAS: Did you say anything to Corporal Payne at this time?

REDFEARN: Not to Corporal Payne, sir, no.

ELIAS: Why not?

REDFEARN: Because I was intimidated and threatened by him, sir.

ELIAS: What, by merely the fact that he was who he was or as a result of something he did or said, or what?

REDFEARN: Merely by the fact that he was a bully, sir.

ELIAS: Did you take it up with anyone?

REDFEARN: Initially I sent for two medics, sir, that never returned.

ELIAS: Sent for two medics?

REDFEARN: Yes, sir.

ELIAS: No response?

REDFEARN: No response, sir.

ELIAS: The medics didn't come?

REDFEARN: Never came, sir.

ELIAS: Let's look at your statement to this Inquiry for a moment. BMI01805, paragraph 134. This is what you say:

'Conditions in the TDF were indescribable.' They were that horrific, were they?

REDFEARN: They were, sir.

ELIAS: 'When the detainees were originally arrested they were tidily dressed and not in any kind of distress. The next time I saw them in the TDF on Monday morning they all looked like they had been in a car crash.'

REDFEARN: Yes, sir.

ELIAS: It was as bad as that, was it?

REDFEARN: It was, sir.

ELIAS: 'The majority of their clothes were ripped and most if not all of them had had heavy bruising across their abdomens and upper arms.' True?

REDFEARN: Yes, sir.

ELIAS: You will go on in the next paragraph in the second line to say: 'Having seen what I had seen, I was "in bits".' What did that mean, Sergeant Redfearn?

REDFEARN: It meant I was upset, sir.

ELIAS: Did the detainees find it difficult, even on that Monday morning, to hold the stress position into which they were being put?

REDFEARN: They were obviously fatigued from being sat like that, sir, no sleep, and they were obviously distressed from the fact that they were hooded and they probably didn't know what was going to happen to them, sir.

ELIAS: Did they find it difficult to remain in the positions in which they were being held?

REDFEARN: Yes, sir.

ELIAS: What would happen if they did fall out of it?

REDFEARN: As soon as they started falling out when I was there, sir, I let them relax as best as I could.

ELIAS: What was Corporal Payne's attitude to allowing detainees to relax in this way?

REDFEARN: He went mad, sir.

ELIAS: In what way?

REDFEARN: He just went absolutely ballistic. I mean, I was not in there at the time, it was after I had been on [guard duty], but he came in and told other members basically that it was not to happen again, or basically what had been happening to the prisoners would happen to them, along them lines, sir.

ELIAS: I want to ask you, please, about Baha Mousa. You were aware of him being taken on a stretcher, were you?

REDFEARN: I was there, sir, yes. When I arrived and by this stage the events were already in full swing, sir.

ELIAS: I want you to tell us what you saw and heard, please.

REDFEARN: Yes, sir. As soon as I got out of the Saxon and I turned the engine off, I heard the screaming, sir, from the middle room. I believe Cooper [was] both shouting and screaming, obviously panicking. There had also been a bad power cut so there was no electricity, no lighting whatsoever, sir. As I entered the [facility], someone passed me a torch, ushered me towards the middle room and that's when I first started seeing the events, sir.

CHAIRMAN: Slowly, please.

ELIAS: Pause there. The shouting or the screaming that you heard was from soldiers, was it?

REDFEARN: Yes, sir. As well as detainees, sir.

ELIAS: You went in. You were handed the torch. You went to the middle room?

REDFEARN: Yes, sir.

ELIAS: What did you see when you got to the middle room?

REDFEARN: I saw Private Cooper and Corporal Payne struggling with a detainee towards the top left-hand side of the middle room, sir.

ELIAS: We know the detainee was Baha Mousa?

REDFEARN: Yes, sir.

ELIAS: In what position was he?

REDFEARN: He was laid flat on the floor. Obviously with Cooper and Corporal Payne on his back, sir.

ELIAS: What did the two soldiers, Cooper and Payne, appear to be doing?

REDFEARN: Panicking, shouting at each other, telling each other what to do. Cooper was saying stuff like, 'I am trying my best'.

ELIAS: What were they trying to do, apparently?

REDFEARN: Trying to get his plasticuffs back on, sir.

ELIAS: Was he hooded at this time?

REDFEARN: Yes, he was, sir.

ELIAS: And what happened?

REDFEARN: He was thrashing about on the floor. He was banging his head off the floor and the wall. I then left to the right-hand side –

CHAIRMAN: Do please take it a bit more slowly.

REDFEARN: I left to the right-hand side, sir, to see what was going on – as soon as there were two soldiers on top of him, sir, I thought that was under control. I then left to the next room to make sure that everything was under control in there, sir. When I re-entered, I saw Corporal Payne, Cooper stood back up –

ELIAS: Take it slowly, if you will.

REDFEARN: They were just stood up, sir, staring at him. I asked what was going on, but straightaway the hood was removed and straightaway you could see that there was something wrong with him, sir.

ELIAS: What told you there was something wrong?

REDFEARN: The fact that one minute he was thrashing about and then the next minute he was just silent, and just by looking at him, sir, I knew that he had stopped breathing.

ELIAS: So what happened?

REDFEARN: I shouted for [a soldier who gave] mouth-to-mouth, sir.

ELIAS: Did that produce any improvement?

REDFEARN: Not at all, sir, no, to be honest.

ELIAS: How long after Baha Mousa was taken away did you learn that he had died?

REDFEARN: Probably within 15 minutes, sir.

ELIAS: That was a great shock, was it, to you?

REDFEARN: It was – it wasn't a shock, sir, no, because the way things had been going it was only going to end one way, sir.

ELIAS: With somebody dying?

REDFEARN: Well, the way things were going, sir, yes.

ELIAS: If it was as bad as that, Sergeant Redfearn, didn't you feel impelled to tell somebody in higher authority that something needed to be done?

REDFEARN: As far as I was aware, sir, everybody in higher authority already knew what was going on, sir.

ELIAS: You had that, you say, from Mr Rodgers?

REDFEARN: And the fact that higher ranking officers had been in there and also the fact that the ops room was ten metres away from the TDF, sir.

ELIAS: You are telling the Chairman and this Inquiry that it became apparent to you that someone was likely to die to the extent that you were not shocked when it happened?

REDFEARN: No, I knew that there was going to be a serious incident, sir.

ELIAS: And yet you still didn't feel that you really had to shout it from the rooftops to somebody?

REDFEARN: There was no one in that camp, sir, as far as I was aware, that I could have told. Even the padre had been in there. If you can't turn to the padre, who can you turn to, sir?

LIEUTENANT CRAIG RODGERS, 11 NOVEMBER 2009

ELIAS: Please give the Inquiry your full name.

RODGERS: Craig Gerard Rodgers.

ELIAS: As far as you were aware, during the time that you were in Iraq, did your multiple do anything which was against the law of armed conflict or in the way of treating civilians in any way improperly?

RODGERS: At the time, I believed not.

ELIAS: Did you have any training before getting to Iraq in the handling of civilian detainees?

RODGERS: Not in the handling of civilians, no.

ELIAS: None at all.

RODGERS: No. The training that we had was based around war fighting, which is the rules that we were working off at the time.

ELIAS: So what was your understanding in relation to the use of hoods?

RODGERS: That any detainees that were believed to be former regime loyalists were to be hooded.

ELIAS: Sorry, why [was it] the former regime loyalists were to be hooded in this way?

RODGERS: We believed it was so they could not see where they were being taken.

ELIAS: So putting it in shorthand, it was a security issue, was it?

RODGERS: It was, yes.

ELIAS: I don't want you to speculate or to guess, Mr Rodgers, but taking the chain above you, do you know of officers above you who were aware of the use of hooding in the ways that you have described in Iraq in 2003?

RODGERS: It was a brigade policy, sir, so every officer in the brigade would have been aware. And I believe that it was also a British forces policy, not just brigade policy.

ELIAS: And what understanding did you have about the rights and wrongs of the use of stress positions?

RODGERS: At the time, sir, I believed it was in accordance with British forces policy. The same as hooding, it was a brigade policy.

ELIAS: When you say it was a brigade policy, was that something that you simply assumed?

RODGERS: It wouldn't have been an assumption, it would have been something I was specifically told. My job in Iraq was to follow orders and I didn't make assumptions, I followed orders that I was given.

ELIAS: And in the arrest and in the period that you were detaining, was there in your mind, Mr Rodgers, any – my words – guiding beacon as to how these individuals, former regime loyalists, if you like, should be treated?

RODGERS: Not that I am aware of.

ELIAS: For example, did you appreciate that you had a duty to treat them – indeed, I suggest all civilian detainees – humanely?

RODGERS: Absolutely, sir.

ELIAS: Where did you get that understanding from?

RODGERS: That's my own moral understanding.

ELIAS: Now, I want to ask you a little about the conditions under which you and the multiple were working in Iraq. You have said in your statement about the nature of the work that you were called upon to carry out. You have indicated that, I think, frequently you would be working 20 hours a day?

RODGERS: Yes, sir.

ELIAS: Did that apply to you or to the multiple, or to both?

RODGERS: I would suggest that applied to every single British soldier in Iraq at the time, sir.

ELIAS: The brief you were given by Corporal Payne with regard to the detainees, to the best of your recollection, what did he tell you?

RODGERS: I can't remember, sir.

ELIAS: Did you see the detainees at this time?

RODGERS: I think I saw them in the room, sir, yes.

ELIAS: Were they in stress positions?

RODGERS: I can't recall, sir.

ELIAS: Were they making any noise?

RODGERS: I can't recall, sir.

ELIAS: Did Corporal Payne show you any injury to any of the detainees at that stage?

RODGERS: He did, sir. He pointed out some bruising to one of the males.

ELIAS: Where was the bruising?

RODGERS: I think it was around his torso, sir.

ELIAS: Why was Corporal Payne pointing out bruising to you at this stage?

RODGERS: I believe it was to point out, sir, that they had been involved in fighting previously.

ELIAS: Why was that relevant to you?

RODGERS: I believe that we had not just wasted our time and arrested people who weren't at least involved in some kind of activity.

ELIAS: So Mr Payne was demonstrating to you that you had picked up men – or a man anyway – who appeared to have been involved in earlier fighting?

RODGERS: I believe so, sir, yes.

ELIAS: What were the conditions in the room itself at that time?

RODGERS: The room was hot, sir, and smelly.

ELIAS: What was the smell?

RODGERS: Just sweat and dirty bodies, sir.

ELIAS: You of course knew Corporal Payne?

RODGERS: I did, sir, yes.

ELIAS: Did he have any reputation?

RODGERS: He was a provost corporal, sir. All provost staff have a reputation as being tough and hard line.

ELIAS: Tough and hard line?

RODGERS: They enforce the policy of the regimental sergeant major for discipline.

ELIAS: So nothing unusual about that?

RODGERS: No, sir.

ELIAS: But – if you forgive me for putting it in shorthand – there was, for whatever reason, open season on these detainees and your [multiple] were permitted to have a pop at them?

RODGERS: No, not at all. Not at all.

ELIAS: You would not have tolerated that under any circumstances, would you?

RODGERS: I would not have tolerated that under any circumstances.

ELIAS: Did you at any time yourself use any violence on any detainee?

RODGERS: Never.

ELIAS: I now want to ask you about what you remember of the events at the time of the death of the detainee, Baha Mousa.
In your statement in October of 2003 you said that [Payne] said: 'There's a problem with one of the prisoners who stopped breathing and has had to go to the medic centre,' or words to that effect. Would that be correct?

RODGERS: If that's what I said, sir, then yes.

ELIAS: Was [Baha Mousa's death] a shock to you?

RODGERS: Yes, sir. It would be a shock to any reasonable human being but I was told by the commanding officer not to ask any questions as it would be a police matter.

Any death in custody – similar to the UK – would be a internal investigation matter and the internal investigation part of the military is the Royal Military Police. I was instructed by the commanding officer not to [ask any questions], and that's a direct order.

ELIAS: Is that the position to this day?

RODGERS: Absolutely, sir.

ELIAS: What did you know about your 'guys trying to fit up Don Payne'?

RODGERS: Nothing, sir. I was not aware of any plot to set up Corporal Payne.

ELIAS: You knew Captain Dai Jones, did you?

RODGERS: I did, sir.

ELIAS: Is it right his death was a very great shock to the whole of 1QLR?

RODGERS: It was a shock, sir, yes.

ELIAS: Did you ever hear any suggestion that the detainees who had been brought in, the Baha Mousa detainees as I call them, had anything to do with the death of Captain Dai Jones?

RODGERS: No, sir.

ELIAS: You certainly heard from one source, did you, at the time – from one source – that these might be people who had killed the RMP?

RODGERS: At that time, sir, I presume Major Peebles told me that on that evening.

CHAIRMAN: 25, you were, at the time. Is that right?

RODGERS: Yes, sir.

CHAIRMAN: What sort of relationship does a young officer have with fairly senior older NCOs?

RODGERS: It varies, sir. There is across the army a common thread that a lot of senior NCOs in particular – the ones that are longer in the tooth – believe that officers have no purpose in the army.

CHAIRMAN: The only other thing I want to ask you about is this: you have no doubt seen the injuries to the detainees, some of which are, to put it mildly, quite horrendous?

RODGERS: Yes, sir.

CHAIRMAN: A number of members of your [multiple] accept that they did punch detainees.

RODGERS: Yes, sir.

CHAIRMAN: You say, as I understand it, that you had no idea that this had happened.

RODGERS: No, sir.

CHAIRMAN: None at all?

RODGERS: None, Sir.

DONALD PAYNE, 16 NOVEMBER 2009

ELIAS: Mr Payne, it is right, isn't it, that you joined the army in 1988?

PAYNE: Yes.

ELIAS: You went straight into 1QLR?

PAYNE: Yes.

ELIAS: At about the turn of the century, 98/99, thereabouts, did you become a regimental policeman?

PAYNE: 1999, yes.

ELIAS: And did you remain on the provost staff until you were discharged from the army following your conviction at the court martial?

PAYNE: Yes.

ELIAS: I want then to begin with your training. At the moment I am dealing, please, with training that was not specifically for provost staff. Hooding: When did you first encounter hooding training in the army?

PAYNE: 1988.

ELIAS: What were you taught about it then?

PAYNE: Just to hood suspects who, you know, we caught, whether in Northern Ireland or in war.

ELIAS: You served in Northern Ireland?

PAYNE: Yes.

ELIAS: To your knowledge were suspects hooded after you joined the army in Northern Ireland?

PAYNE: If caught, yes.

ELIAS: Were you told what the purpose of hooding detainees was at that stage?

PAYNE: To disorientate them.

ELIAS: Did you receive any what I might call general training in how detainees, prisoners of war or detainees, were to be treated if captured?

45

PAYNE: We used to see a video once a year.

ELIAS: What, if anything, was the general message of that video as you remember it?

PAYNE: To treat them properly.

ELIAS: By 'properly', what do you mean?

PAYNE: Feed them, water them, make sure that they were safe.

ELIAS: Were you told that minimum force was to be the rule?

PAYNE: Yes.

ELIAS: Is there any doubt but that you would have known at the time of the events this Inquiry is concerned with that civilians must be treated humanely at all times?

PAYNE: Yes.

ELIAS: No doubt about that, is there?

PAYNE: No doubt.

ELIAS: Thank you. Was that something which you knew that the detainees in Iraq were entitled to?

PAYNE: No.

ELIAS: What did you believe that they were entitled to that differed from that care?

PAYNE: I don't understand your question.

ELIAS: Why did –

PAYNE: I didn't know any of this in Iraq. When we went to Iraq it was a new thing for everybody.

ELIAS: Yes. What I am asking you, Mr Payne, and I thought you were agreeing with me, was that as far as the detainees in Iraq were concerned you would have understood that they were entitled to be treated humanely, that is to say with respect, with fairness.

PAYNE: Yes.

ELIAS: Is that right?

PAYNE: Yes.

ELIAS: You would have appreciated that at the time, but I think you would agree now, would you, they plainly were not treated humanely, were they?

PAYNE: No, they weren't.

ELIAS: You refer in your statement to this Inquiry to training you were given in Catterick.

PAYNE: Yes.

ELIAS: Were there lectures, talks?

PAYNE: It was a 40-minute lecture.

ELIAS: Who gave it?

PAYNE: Two guys from the Intelligence Corps.

ELIAS: What was the content of the talk?

PAYNE: Basically it was on tactical questioning, to get them questioned as fast and as soon as we could.

ELIAS: What else were you taught?

PAYNE: Nothing.

ELIAS: If you look at where you refer to this training, you say it was a two-hour lecture given by the Intelligence Corps to senior NCOs. Your statement goes on: '... lack of sleep and to keep prisoners confused as much as we could.'

PAYNE: Yes.

ELIAS: Was anything said as to what the purpose of that was: Shock of capture, lack of sleep?

PAYNE: It was to aid the tactical questioner, or the interrogator.

ELIAS: Was anything at that lecture – and I don't want you to guess if you don't remember, Mr Payne – was anything at that lecture, that session, said about hooding or stress positions?

PAYNE: Not about stress positions, no.

ELIAS: Was anything said about hooding?

PAYNE: Yes.

ELIAS: What was that?

PAYNE: They were to be hooded.

ELIAS: Was anything said about the duration of hooding?

PAYNE: No.

ELIAS: Before you went out to Iraq, what was your position in relation to the use of stress positions on detainees? Was it appropriate or not?

PAYNE: We didn't know we'd be dealing with detainees, so I didn't have a position.

ELIAS: Where did responsibility lie for the detainees?

PAYNE: With Major Peebles, the overall –

ELIAS: Sorry? You are just dropping your voice a little.

PAYNE: The BGIRO [battlegroup internment review officer] was overall in charge.

ELIAS: Now, in relation to the manner in which detainees were to be treated and in accordance with what you say was the s.o.p. [standard operating procedure] can you help us, please, as to who was aware of that in the chain of command through you?

PAYNE: Everybody.

ELIAS: How did it go?

PAYNE: All the way up.

ELIAS: To whom?

PAYNE: The CO.

ELIAS: On Sunday – the day of their arrest and their being brought to the TDF – who was in charge?

PAYNE: Myself.

ELIAS: They arrive, they are met one by one, you say, by you. You search them. What happens to them when they are searched?

PAYNE: The plasticuffs are removed from the back and placed out in front.

ELIAS: What else?

PAYNE: Sandbags are reapplied.

ELIAS: Who applied the sandbags?

PAYNE: Me.

ELIAS: How many?

PAYNE: One.

ELIAS: We know that these detainees were detained until the Tuesday morning at some time when they were sent off to Umm Qasr.

PAYNE: Yes.

ELIAS: In that 48 hours or so, for what period of time did the hoods remain on these detainees?

PAYNE: 36 hours.

ELIAS: Until a particular event?

PAYNE: Yes.

ELIAS: What was that?

PAYNE: Death of Baha Mousa.

ELIAS: You have told us that you had them brought in one by one? Let's deal with the initial six. Was it apparent to you that some of these – and I hope I am not putting it too delicately – were older rather than younger?

PAYNE: Yes, they was old men, yes.

ELIAS: You put them into plasticuffs and hoods. Were they put immediately into stress positions?

PAYNE: Yes.

ELIAS: What was the stress position?

PAYNE: Back against the wall, knees bent.

ELIAS: Arms out in front of them?

PAYNE: Yes.

ELIAS: And they were expected to hold that position?

PAYNE: Yes.

ELIAS: Throughout the period that these detainees were in that detention centre – the 48 hours or so – who in authority to your knowledge – I don't want you to guess about it – knew of their presence there?

PAYNE: Everybody.

ELIAS: Meaning?

PAYNE: CO [Colonel Mendonca].

ELIAS: Mr Peebles?

PAYNE: Yes.

ELIAS: You say the CO. How did you know that he knew?

PAYNE: Because he would have to be informed.

ELIAS: Thank you. Over that period of time, emanating from the TDF would there have been shouting and screaming?

PAYNE: Yes.

ELIAS: Who would have been doing the shouting?

PAYNE: Myself, if I was there, and the guard.

ELIAS: Why would you have shouted?

PAYNE: To keep them awake.

ELIAS: Shouting of a kind that would have been heard – might have been heard – in, for example, the accommodation block opposite?

PAYNE: Yes.

ELIAS: Did your conduct in fact include kicking and punching –

PAYNE: Yes.

ELIAS: – routinely to detainees?

PAYNE: Yes.

ELIAS: And in relation to these detainees, the Baha Mousa detainees, why did you involve yourself in kicking and punching them?

PAYNE: No reason.

ELIAS: For no reason. I just want you to think about it. I am not suggesting it for one moment, but was it the case, for example, that you believed that they were involved in some previous killing?

PAYNE: Maybe, yes.

ELIAS: Was that something that had anything to do with your behaviour?

PAYNE: Yes. I think it was because we thought they had murdered the RMP[s].

ELIAS: Who is the 'we' in that sentence?

PAYNE: Everybody.

ELIAS: You go on in the statement to say this: 'Moreover at one time or another I saw all the members of the multiple emulate me.'

PAYNE: Yes.

ELIAS: Is that true?

PAYNE: Yes.

ELIAS: Why haven't you said that before?

PAYNE: Misguided loyalties.

ELIAS: You lied about almost everything, didn't you?

PAYNE: Yes.

ELIAS: We can go to innumerable other examples where you told the police investigating you had never assaulted any of them and you had never seen any such assaults, can't we?

PAYNE: Yes.

ELIAS: Your interview under caution on 9 March 2004. You were asked about the choir. You prodded detainees who made noises one after the other?

PAYNE: That was one of my checks when I came in to the detention –

ELIAS: To see if they were awake, you said?

PAYNE: Yes.

ELIAS: I am going to ask you, please, to look at a few photographs with me of some of the detainees, photographs taken a day or two after they left the TDF at Umm Qasr. Injury to the left flank, bruising. Do you know how those injuries were come by?

PAYNE: By being punched and kicked.

ELIAS: Should the Inquiry now understand that you will have kicked and punched each of these detainees?

PAYNE: Yes.

ELIAS: Forceful blows?

PAYNE: Yes.

ELIAS: Designed to hurt them?

PAYNE: Yes.

ELIAS: Injury to the nose of D003. Do you know how such injuries were occasioned?

PAYNE: No.

ELIAS: Were sandbags rubbed across their faces?

PAYNE: No, not by me.

ELIAS: Was there any eye gouging, moving of sandbags in that way?

PAYNE: No.

ELIAS: Grabbing around the face?

PAYNE: Yes.

ELIAS: You did that, did you?

PAYNE: Yes.

ELIAS: Grabbing around the face for what purpose?

PAYNE: To lift the head up.

ELIAS: In doing that, could you, if you like, have scuffed the bag across, for example, the nose of the detainee?

PAYNE: It could have happened, yes.

ELIAS: Why did you grab the head to lift up?

PAYNE: If the head had slumped.

ELIAS: If they were falling asleep or something?

PAYNE: Yes.

ELIAS: We see bruising and marking to the torso of D003's body. Would that have been kicking and punching too?

PAYNE: Yes.

ELIAS: When you saw others from the multiple kicking and punching, where were their kicks and punches directed?

PAYNE: Various parts.

ELIAS: Being?

PAYNE: Various parts.

ELIAS: What do you mean by 'various parts'?

PAYNE: Various parts of their body.

ELIAS: Yes, which parts?

PAYNE: Various parts.

ELIAS: Well, which parts?

PAYNE: I cannot be specific.

ELIAS: The feet?

PAYNE: Yes.

ELIAS: The knees?

PAYNE: Various parts.

ELIAS: The thighs?

PAYNE: Various parts.

ELIAS: The trunk?

PAYNE: Various parts.

ELIAS: The head? What, any? Any and all, is –

PAYNE: Yes.

ELIAS: – that what you are saying?

PAYNE: Yes.

ELIAS: Would you agree, Mr Payne, that it would seem to be apparent from photographs – forget any other evidence – that these detainees who suffered those injuries were not subjected to the odd kick or punch, were they?

PAYNE: Yes.

ELIAS: You would agree?

PAYNE: Yes.

ELIAS: You say, you told us, that you couldn't see, didn't see, any injury on any of them at any time up until and including the death of Baha Mousa, correct?

PAYNE: Yes.

ELIAS: What you said was – can I remind you: 'I could see the prisoners were being worn down, they were knackered through lack of sleep and having been in the stress positions for a long time.'

PAYNE: Yes.

ELIAS: That was very obvious to you, was it?

PAYNE: Yes.

ELIAS: And very obviously inhumane?

PAYNE: Yes.

ELIAS: Was that a matter that troubled you?

PAYNE: Yes.

ELIAS: Did you take it up with anybody?

PAYNE: Yes.

ELIAS: With whom?

PAYNE: The BGIRO.

ELIAS: Mr Peebles?

PAYNE: Yes.

ELIAS: At what stage did you take it up?

PAYNE: After the Tactical Questions had finished.

ELIAS: Tell us what transpired.

PAYNE: I was told [they were wanted] with the shock of capture still because they had intelligence to give.

ELIAS: So it was an explicit order, was it, to maintain the stress positions?

PAYNE: Yes.

ELIAS: And hooding?

PAYNE: Yes.

ELIAS: And you say that came from Major Peebles?

PAYNE: Yes.

ELIAS: From that time of assaulting the detainees on the Sunday evening through until the death of Baha Mousa, should the Inquiry understand – tell me this is wrong if it is – from your evidence that more or less whenever you went back to the TDF you would involve yourself in more violence of this kind?

PAYNE: Yes.

ELIAS: And you saw members of the multiple using violence?

PAYNE: Yes.

ELIAS: Punching and kicking?

PAYNE: Yes.

ELIAS: Would that be the guard on duty?

PAYNE: Yes.

ELIAS: When, if at all, were you first aware that Baha Mousa was, if you like, causing any problems?

PAYNE: Sunday teatime.

ELIAS: What were the problems?

PAYNE: He kept getting out of his plasticuffs and taking his hood off.

ELIAS: So was any decision come to as to how this problem was to be overcome or dealt with?

PAYNE: Yes, we was to place him in the middle room.

ELIAS: What were you told, if anything, to do with him in the middle room?

PAYNE: To plasticuff his thumbs together and his little fingers and place him laid down on the floor with his chin in his hands.

ELIAS: So on his stomach?

PAYNE: Yes.

ELIAS: And was he so plasticuffed, fingers and thumbs as well as wrists?

PAYNE: Yes.

ELIAS: Then placed on the floor?

PAYNE: Yes.

ELIAS: Did that solve the problem?

PAYNE: It seemed to, yes.

ELIAS: So now moving onto [the night one day later], the incident relating to his death.

PAYNE: Yes.

ELIAS: Well, then, please tell us what happened in this incident: where did you first encounter Baha Mousa?

PAYNE: Just inside the left-hand room.

ELIAS: So he was what, in the doorway, if you like, of the left-hand room, is that what you are saying, coming out of the small room?

PAYNE: Yes.

ELIAS: Hooded, plasticuffed?

PAYNE: No hood.

ELIAS: What was he doing?

PAYNE: Walking towards the door.

ELIAS: What did he do then?

PAYNE: He saw me. I screamed – well, shouted – that he was trying to escape. He then turned and I followed him, got him down to the floor in the middle room.

ELIAS: What happened there?

PAYNE: I placed my knee in the small of his knee at the back. Put my hand across his face, pulled him back, and knelt with my knee to push him forward. Got him to the ground. By this time Cooper came and helped me.

ELIAS: Had you been calling for help?

PAYNE: Yes.

ELIAS: Did you use any further force upon him other than that which you used to take him to the ground and hold his arms together?

PAYNE: Yes, I had my knee in his back.

ELIAS: Why did you have your knee in his back?

PAYNE: To control him.

ELIAS: In the thrashing about, do you say that any part of his body struck anything or anybody?

PAYNE: I heard his head, but I don't know whether it was the floor or the wall.

ELIAS: What did you hear his head?

PAYNE: I heard it whack.

ELIAS: What sort of a noise was it?

PAYNE: Like a whack.

ELIAS: Did that bang either to the wall or the floor stop the thrashing about?

PAYNE: Yes.

ELIAS: What happened after that?

PAYNE: I reapplied the plasticuffs. We sat him up. Cooper had checked for a pulse. He had a pulse, but I sent somebody to get the – a medic.

ELIAS: Mr Payne, It has been said that in the course of that incident you lost your temper and kicked out and punched out at Baha Mousa. Is that right?

PAYNE: No.

ELIAS: You didn't lose it and go into a sort of frenzy?

PAYNE: No.

ELIAS: When you realised that there was something wrong, did you stay with him or did you move away?

PAYNE: Moved away.

ELIAS: Why?

PAYNE: To let the doctor and the medic get there.

ELIAS: Subsequently, did you say anything to them about what had happened?

PAYNE: I was explaining it all to the adjutant. And I just kept saying, 'I can't believe he's dead. He only banged his head.'

ELIAS: 'He only banged his head'. Did you say anything to those members of the Rodgers multiple or, indeed, any other to the effect that it should be said that he only banged his head?

PAYNE: No.

ELIAS: In the sense of meaning 'we all know that worse than that happened, but that's the story we are going to tell'?

PAYNE: No, I never said that –

ELIAS: Nothing of that kind was said by you, was it?

PAYNE: No.

ELIAS: Can I then move on to just a couple of other aspects of the 48 hours that we have been talking about. Going back to your statement which you signed today, you referred to an incident involving Lieutenant Rodgers.

PAYNE: Yes.

ELIAS: Can you just tell us what happened, please?

PAYNE: It was early on the Monday morning. I came in to check on them to make sure that they got their breakfast, and the multiple was there, Mr Rodgers was in the middle room with the – the young lad. There was a open jerry can there in front of him.

ELIAS: Say again?

PAYNE: An open jerry can of petrol there in front of him.

ELIAS: In front of whom?

PAYNE: The young lad, so he could smell the fumes.

ELIAS: Was the young lad, as you call him, hooded at the time?

PAYNE: Yes, hooded.

ELIAS: What happened?

PAYNE: He poured water over him, took the jerry can of water away, removed the hood and then lit a match as if he was going to burn him.

ELIAS: So who poured water over him?

PAYNE: Rodgers.

ELIAS: Who lit the match?

PAYNE: Rodgers.

ELIAS: When you observed that, did you say anything to Rodgers or any other member of the multiple about it?

PAYNE: No.

ELIAS: Why not?

PAYNE: Because he's an officer.

ELIAS: So the match is lit. What happened then?

PAYNE: The young lad went hysterical.

ELIAS: How did it end?

PAYNE: I can't remember.

ELIAS: I will be corrected if I am wrong about it, I don't recall the young man suggesting that that happened to him. It did, did it?

PAYNE: Yes.

ELIAS: Not something that you are making up against Mr Rodgers or the Rodgers multiple?

PAYNE: No.

ELIAS: Did you ever have any conversation with the CO about what had happened –

PAYNE: Yes.

ELIAS: – to these detainees or to Baha Mousa?

PAYNE: Yes.

ELIAS: What did you tell him?

PAYNE: What had happened.

ELIAS: What you have told us?

PAYNE: Yes.

ELIAS: As to the struggle?

PAYNE: Yes.

ELIAS: What did he say to that?

PAYNE: He said, 'I hope it's right, because if it's not' – well, 'I hope it's right, because if it's not it's the end of my career and your career.'

ELIAS: What did you understand him to be saying by that?

PAYNE: That it was either me or him.

MICHAEL PEEBLES, 7 DECEMBER 2009

ELIAS: Sir, I call Michael Edwin Peebles, Major Peebles, please.

CHAIRMAN: Yes. If you would be kind enough to stand, as you are, Major, I will ask you to take the oath.
MICHAEL EDWIN PEEBLES (sworn)

CHAIRMAN: Please sit down, and if you would be kind enough to speak into the microphone, then hopefully we will all be able to hear you.

ELIAS: I want to ask you specifically about your BGIRO role.

PEEBLES: Yes, sir.

ELIAS: Had you ever heard of the role of BGIRO before you went to Iraq?

PEEBLES: No, I had not, sir.

ELIAS: When you were appointed to that role, what did you understand was that role and its responsibility?

PEEBLES: I understood it principally, sir, to be a quasi-judicial appointment in the sense that I had to come to a decision as to whether a detainee that had been brought in was to be released back into the population, handed over to the police force or sent down to the T.I.F. [Theatre Internment Facility at Umm Qasr] for further questioning and for prolonged custody.

ELIAS: So you took the internment decision?

PEEBLES: Yes, sir, I did.

ELIAS: Who had responsibility for detainees brought into BG main?

PEEBLES: In terms of looking after the detainees, the regimental police staff, were there to do that specific task.

ELIAS: Who had, ultimately, as you understood it, the responsibility for them?

PEEBLES: Overall? Overall, that would then go back to the commanding officer.

ELIAS: Yes.

PEEBLES: I had – there is no doubt I had a pivotal role over the co-ordination of dealing with the detainees, but in terms of the sole responsibility for the handling and welfare of detainees, I don't believe that came down to me, if that is the question.

ELIAS: Major Peebles, you are answering my question before I ask it, but let's deal with it since you have. You had a pivotal role in handling or dealing with the detainees? What was that pivotal role, please?

PEEBLES: That role in terms of – bringing in the evidence and coming to a decision as to what –

ELIAS: I am sorry to stop you, just so we make some progress. What was your role specifically in relation to what we might all understand as the handling of the detainees? If something was being done wrong, you would seek to correct it?

PEEBLES: Yes, I would.

ELIAS: Just dealing with the practicalities, if you like, of operating your role pre-Operation Salerno. You understand what I think, in this Inquiry, we have been calling the '14-hour rule', did you?

PEEBLES: Yes, I did.

ELIAS: What did that mean?

PEEBLES: That meant that we should try to get the detainees or internees down to the theatre internment facility [at Umm Qasr] within 14 hours.

ELIAS: Let me move on to Operation Salerno itself, then, please. You knew that prisoners had to be treated humanely –

PEEBLES: Yes, sir.

ELIAS: – and in accordance with the Geneva Conventions?

PEEBLES: Yes, sir.

ELIAS: You obviously knew that they had to be treated lawfully, that is to say for the purposes of this Inquiry anyway, not assaulted.

PEEBLES: Yes, sir.

ELIAS: You believed that conditioning was approved at brigade level, if not higher?

PEEBLES: Yes, I did.

ELIAS: And you saw yourself [as] having some general oversight where conditioning was being used to ensure that guards or provost staff were not going over the top?

PEEBLES: Yes, I think that's quite natural.

ELIAS: Did you visit the TDF when the Operation Salerno detainees were there on the Sunday, Monday and Tuesday?

PEEBLES: On the Sunday and Monday, yes sir.

ELIAS: Do you recall, over that period, how many visits you made to the TDF?

PEEBLES: I think it was approximately three to four on the Sunday and three on the Monday prior to the incident of the death.

ELIAS: Prior to the death of Baha Mousa?

PEEBLES: Yes.

ELIAS: So about seven visits?

PEEBLES: That would be approximately correct, sir, yes.

ELIAS: So that state of affairs, the conditioning, the hooding, the stress positions and so on, looking at matters now, Major Peebles, do you accept any responsibility for the detainees being subjected to conditioning over that period?

PEEBLES: I think it was part of the process and therefore I was involved in that process, but I don't accept full responsibility but –

ELIAS: But you accept some, do you?

PEEBLES: In part, yes. I was aware of the practice, yes, sir, and indeed I condoned it.

ELIAS: Did you go further than simply condoning it? Did you at any stage instruct that conditioning should be commenced?

PEEBLES: Yes, I did. I suggested it should start at about 16.30 hours [on the Sunday].

ELIAS: You ordered the guard to start conditioning?

PEEBLES: Yes.

ELIAS: When you gave that order, did you see whether they put it into operation?

PEEBLES: Yes, I am sure that they did. They were – I didn't hang around for that long but I saw them go in, shout at the detainees to get up and to get their hands up, i.e. to –

ELIAS: They were already hooded?

PEEBLES: Yes, sir.

ELIAS: Wasn't that part of the conditioning?

PEEBLES: Well, yes, it is, it is, but the hoods were – the hoods remained on for – the hoods remained on in that period because we felt that maybe they posed a potential threat and therefore the hooding was appropriate.

ELIAS: I think you say in your statement to this Inquiry that you became aware of the medical assessment having been carried out at 3 o'clock in the afternoon –

PEEBLES: Yes.

ELIAS: – by which time the detainees had been in army custody for six or seven hours or so.

PEEBLES: Yes, sir, they had.

ELIAS: Wasn't that something that concerned you?

PEEBLES: We had to wait for the tactical questioners [to arrive] and the questioning clearly wasn't going to happen for some time. We had a lot of information to sift through, a lot of documentation, et cetera. So I suppose there was – there could have been – there could have been an assumption on Corporal Payne's part – time for him to co-ordinate the medical visit. I wasn't sat there, honestly, just doing nothing and twiddling my thumbs, but –

ELIAS: Time for Corporal Payne to co-ordinate the medical visit? What was involved in this co-ordination?

PEEBLES: I presume he would go down to the regimental aid post and call for some medics to come and do the examination.

ELIAS: About 80 metres away?

PEEBLES: Yes, not far at all. It should have happened sooner, I plainly admit to you. I think it could have happened very quickly, but, for whatever reason, it appears that it didn't.

ELIAS: You know [Corporal Payne] told the Inquiry what he did?

PEEBLES: Yes, I am aware of that, sir, yes.

ELIAS: Routinely returning and gratuitously assaulting – unlawfully kicking and punching detainees. You never saw or heard anything of that kind?

PEEBLES: No, I didn't, sir. As I say, I hardly saw Corporal Payne over those two days, but obviously when a problem arose, he came and told me about it.

ELIAS: We are coming to the Baha Mousa incident in due course. So you have started the conditioning process, you say. You never called it off?

PEEBLES: No, not formally, no, sir.

ELIAS: Why, that Sunday afternoon, did you pass on the fact that you believed that these detainees might have something to do with the deaths of the three [Royal Military Police] men?

PEEBLES: Sir, I was either asked or I said in terms of passing on information to the guard that – I was either asked why these people were in custody, so I gave a brief explanation, or I just said it. It wasn't to – it was so that they were fully informed. I said, 'The reason we are questioning them is because we might believe that they would know something about the RMP incident'. I never said – well, you know, I never said that they were responsible because clearly, at that stage, we didn't know that.

ELIAS: Wasn't it highly irresponsible, to put it at its lowest, to spread the rumour that detainees being guarded by soldiers of 1QLR – wasn't it highly irresponsible to spread that possibility as a rumour?

PEEBLES: No, I thought it was appropriate that they know the people who we were dealing with, that they were a potential threat and –

ELIAS: Major Peebles, why did they need to know that?

PEEBLES: Sorry, sir?

ELIAS: Why did they have to know that these men might have something to do with the death of three RMPs?

PEEBLES: Well, sir, they may have been a potential threat. That's all. It's part of a briefing process, sir. You try to inform people.

ELIAS: Of course what you could have said to anybody who enquired is, 'Mind your own business'?

PEEBLES: Sir, they are responsible for dealing – for looking after detainees, and they have a right to know. If anybody escaped or tried to escape, et cetera, they should – you know, they should be aware of the type of people potentially they were dealing with. I didn't say to them – I certainly didn't say to them that they were responsible for. I did make it clear that we believe there might be an involvement.

ELIAS: It wasn't the case, was it, that by late on the Sunday evening, it was, for these detainees – if I'll be forgiven for [putting] it this way – open house on assaulting them because of that?

PEEBLES: With some of the evidence which has come out of here, I would agree that they found motive. It doesn't justify it though, sir, whatever you believe.

ELIAS: No. I suppose the question remains, doesn't it, Major Peebles why did you contribute in spreading that story?

PEEBLES: I did not want to spread a story, sir, and certainly, if I felt that it would result in such behaviour, I wouldn't have said anything.

ELIAS: What role did you play in the [Tactical Questioning]?

PEEBLES: I – there would be – I would take notes. I would – if there was guidance that needed providing, I would also look at whatever previous notes had been written, so I could feed questions into the tactical questioner if so required.

ELIAS: Do you recall one of those detainees being particularly young?

PEEBLES: I do, yes. D005.

ELIAS: Was he treated in any different way to the other detainees so far as tactical questioning is concerned?

PEEBLES: No, except for the way that he was placed outside, next to the generator, yes.

ELIAS: So D005 was placed next to the generator?

PEEBLES: Between questioning sessions, yes.

ELIAS: Who ordered that he be placed next to the generator between questioning sessions?

PEEBLES: I think it was the tactical questioner, but it wasn't – it was to place him somewhere where he could be put directly –

ELIAS: We will come to the reasons, Major Peebles, in a moment.

PEEBLES: But I was aware of that –

CHAIRMAN: Just listen to the question.

ELIAS: Did you give the order that D005 be put by the generator?

PEEBLES: I can't recall specifically giving an order of that nature.

ELIAS: Does that mean that it might have been you who did?

PEEBLES: It might well have been.

ELIAS: What was the purpose of putting D005 to the generator?

PEEBLES: The purpose of putting him there was that he was being fairly non-responsive to the first few questions that he was being asked.
It was more practical to send him just outside, which was close by where the generator was, then [he] could be brought back in within a few minutes for further questioning.

ELIAS: What, so this was merely an operation for convenience's sake, was it?

PEEBLES: Yes, yes.

ELIAS: Not, for example, to punish D005 because he wasn't being cooperative in answering questions?

PEEBLES: No.

ELIAS: No?

PEEBLES: I wouldn't say that it was punishment. The guy was already pretty scared. I saw him in interview. It was more a matter of practicality.

ELIAS: When he was placed by the generator, [was he] hooded?

PEEBLES: Yes, I believe he was.

ELIAS: Plasticuffed?

PEEBLES: Yes.

ELIAS: A guard with him?

PEEBLES: He either had a guard with him or there was a guard by the doorway. I don't know if there was a guard right next to him, actually.

ELIAS: The impression one gets, Major Peebles – correct me if I'm wrong – is that that was the plan with this detainee, that there would be a short session of questioning, he would be told to get out, taken out and brought back in. Was that the plan for him?

PEEBLES: Yes, I think it was – a sort of a naughty schoolboy routine, I think.

ELIAS: So when he was taken to the generator, you would now concede, would you, that it was part of what I might call 'unofficial conditioning' in his case?

PEEBLES: No, I would say it was a place to put him.

ELIAS: It was a punishment for him, wasn't it?

PEEBLES: It wasn't – the generator was not a punishment. The naughty boy syndrome is a way in which – what I am explaining is the way in which the tactical questioner acted with the individual involved, as a schoolmaster would at school.

ELIAS: And the generator was very hot?

PEEBLES: Sir, not for that reason, no.

ELIAS: But it was, wasn't it?

PEEBLES: The generator was hot, the conditions were hot and, as far as I'm aware, he wasn't placed right up against it.

ELIAS: The generator was noisy, wasn't it?

PEEBLES: It was noisy, yes.

ELIAS: These were not reasons that he was put there, were they?

PEEBLES: No, sir.

ELIAS: That is the truth, is it?

PEEBLES: That is the truth. It was convenient.

NICHOLAS JUSTIN MERCER

CHAIRMAN: Yes. Good morning, ladies and gentlemen. It may not have escaped the notice of the more alert of you that the Inquiry has not been able to get email in the last few days. I'm told that there's a problem in the Holborn area. BT are doing their best to resolve it. At the moment they have not resolved it and it's not certain when they will. However at around about lunchtime today, I hope that you will be notified of an alternative method of getting emails to the Inquiry through what I'm told is termed a 'solicitor's box' by another method. So I hope that will assist. As to when BT manage to get us back on our own email, I have no idea and I don't think, sadly they have.

ELIAS: Then I will call, if I may, Nicholas Justin Mercer, please. Colonel Mercer, please.

CHAIRMAN: Colonel, would you be kind enough to stand up, please, whilst I ask that take the oath?

NICHOLAS JUSTIN MERCER (sworn)

ELIAS: Would you give the Inquiry your full name, please?

MERCER: Nicholas Justin Mercer.

ELIAS: Your current rank is lieutenant colonel.

MERCER: Correct.

ELIAS: I want to begin, please, by briefly asking you about your role in Iraq in 2003.

MERCER: Well, I was legal adviser for the 1st Armoured Division. I gave legal advice to the chain of command on all matters pertaining to military operations.

ELIAS: You have undertaken training in the law of armed conflict yourself, have you?

MERCER: Yes, I have.

ELIAS: That involved learning about the appropriate treatment of prisoners of war, amongst other things?

MERCER: Yes.

ELIAS: If there was a single message that emerged from that training in relation to the handling of prisoners of war, what was it?

MERCER: Well I use the phrase 'humanity and dignity'.

ELIAS: May I come, then, please, to training that you may have given in relation to Op Telic 1 [the overall operation in Iraq]. You say in the statement to this Inquiry – I don't think it need be put up, but it's your paragraph 17 – that all soldiers regardless of rank are supposed to receive annual training in the law of armed conflict.

MERCER: That's correct.

ELIAS: Paragraph 20 of your statement – you say this: '... given the training provided, I had no concerns about prisoner-handling prior to deployment as I believed it was well understood by all members of the division.'
By that the Inquiry should understand that you were saying you believed it was well understood that prisoners should be treated with humanity and dignity.

MERCER: Yes, I mean, this message is reiterated the whole time. The video that soldiers watch each year, which is a sort of old cold war relic or it was then, makes it absolutely clear: do not mistreat prisoners. This message is repeated and repeated and repeated.

ELIAS: At the time of your deployment to Iraq, what was your understanding about the rights and wrongs of the use of hoods on prisoners?

MERCER: I didn't even give it any thought because I just didn't envisage it. It hadn't happened [in the first Gulf War], so why would I have it in contemplation? It just didn't emerge – you know, it wasn't an issue.

ELIAS: So you were aware that hooding had been, can I put it this way in shorthand, ruled as being inhumane?

MERCER: Well, in contravention of the Convention on Human Rights, yes.

ELIAS: Thank you. Were you aware, prior to deployment to Iraq, that hooding was being used for any purpose?

MERCER: No, none whatsoever.

ELIAS: Would your view of the use of stress positions have been: 'They are off the menu entirely and not to be used under any circumstances'?

MERCER: Of course, both under Geneva and under the European Convention on Human Rights.

ELIAS: You say at paragraph 23: 'Although the UK maintained that it took its responsibilities under the Geneva Convention in relation to prisoners very seriously, this was not my experience. In my view, the issue of prisoners had very low priority and was treated more as an inconvenience than an obligation under international law.'

MERCER: Yes, I think that's correct.

ELIAS: If I may comment, that's quite a serious allegation to be making.

MERCER: It is. It's to do with resources. If you don't resource it properly, it is a low priority.

ELIAS: Could we have a look, please, at paragraph 21 of your second statement? We find that at BMI06901A paragraph 21. If we just go down three or four lines in the paragraph, you say this: 'However hooding was not banned by Permanent Joint Headquarters until after Baha Mousa's death and emails in May 2004 show that there was an information gap within the MoD about the practice of hooding.
Can we just look at the documents. MOD028354. A loose minute that's dated 25 November [1999]. 'Legal status of interrogation in situations other than general war.' 'The use of five interrogation techniques, i.e. keeping detainees' heads covered by a hood, continuous and monotonous noise, sleep deprivation, deprivation of food and water and making the detainees stand' essentially in stress positions ... 'amounted to inhuman and degrading treatment.'

Your reference to those documents in 1999 was a reference, was it, to the fact that there appears from that correspondence to be an indication that, for example, hooding was not to be employed?

MERCER: That's correct. It's clear that advice was sought in 1999 and the army made it very clear that these [five techniques] were prohibited. Then we bump into the issue again in 2003.

As soon as I saw hooding in the Joint Field Interrogation Team, I wrote immediately to the General [Officer Commanding] Robin Brims –

ELIAS: We are going to come to that.

MERCER: The point is, sir, that when I saw it for the first time, I put in an immediate complaint.

ELIAS: I want to ask you, please, about visits [in 2003] that you made to the [Joint Field Interrogation Team]. You kept a diary. Was that a diary intended for your own use, your own consumption, if you like, alone?

MERCER: Yes, my grandfather had kept one in 1939, so I rather wanted to repeat what he had done, so it was just personal.

CHAIRMAN: You have always kept a diary, have you?

MERCER: No, I've never kept a diary. I don't like them.

CHAIRMAN: Never.

MERCER: But I thought these were historic times.

CHAIRMAN: So this is a new departure for you?

MERCER: Yes.

ELIAS: What I really wanted to know, Colonel, was whether you were keeping a diary with a view to it being published to a wider audience.

MERCER: No, it was a private record and my wife very kindly typed it up at the end for me.

ELIAS: It was never intended to be anything more than that, was it?

MERCER: No. Quite frankly some of it is embarrassing.

ELIAS: When you say 'typed up' out of pure curiosity, does that mean that what we see as your diary in that rather neat writing is a font?

MERCER: It's a font, yes.

CHAIRMAN: I was for a moment lost with envy of anyone who is able to write as carefully as that, but …

ELIAS: If we look at your diary, please, can we look at 28 March [2003]. You refer to this, don't you, in the last half a dozen lines of this entry? 'I went by helicopter with General Brims to Umm Qasr to see the prisoner of war collation area.' Is that the occasion that you are now referring to?

MERCER: That would be correct, yes.

ELIAS: You say: '... a unique experience where I saw over 3,000 prisoners of war all in different compounds separated by large strands of barbed wire. Very few were in uniform, but all had been captured in various battles over the last seven days. Some looked terrified, others defiant.' Just before we go on, then, on that occasion who else apart from yourself and General Brims was present at the JFIT?

MERCER: We weren't going to see the [Joint Field Interrogation Team].

ELIAS: No.

MERCER: We were going to visit the Prisoner of War Camp.

ELIAS: I understand.

MERCER: The JFIT was situated at the entrance to the prisoner of war camp; in other words, as you walked into the camp, the JFIT was to your right and there was a guard on the gate. The General was met by a huge posse of people and I sort of tagged along at the back.

ELIAS: And what, if anything, did you see that caused you [to] have concern?

MERCER: Well, this was the first time that I'd seen what was going on [in the JFIT]. As I walked past, I saw two lines of prisoners, all kneeling in the sand, hands cuffed behind their backs, all with hoods on their heads.

ELIAS: All of them hooded. With what?

MERCER: Well, I saw sandbags on their heads and I'm pretty sure there were other bags as well...I mean, it's a bit like seeing a picture of Guantanamo Bay for the first time. It is quite a shock.

ELIAS: Would you describe the position in which the prisoners were being held – apart from the hoods on their heads – would you describe the positions as being stress positions?

MERCER: Yes, I mean I wrote – you have got my memo to General Brims.

ELIAS: We are going to come to that.

MERCER: If I just go back to the stress positions, the prisoners were cuffed behind their backs, up like this (indicates), so it looked extremely uncomfortable.

ELIAS: Did you speak to anyone as to what was going on?

MERCER: I did, I expressed my concern as to what was happening and my view that it was illegal.

ELIAS: So you sent this memo. Paragraph 6, please, where you say this: 'I visited the [JFIT] and witnessed a number of prisoners of war who were hooded and in various stress positions. I am informed that this is in accordance with British Army doctrine on tactical questioning.
'Whereas it may be in accordance with British Army doctrine (you went on to say), in my opinion, it violates international law. Prisoners of war must at all times be protected against acts of violence or intimidation and must have respect for their persons and their honour (you refer to Articles 13 and 14 of Geneva Convention III). I accept that tactical questioning may be permitted but this behaviour clearly violates the Convention.' If we look at paragraph 43 of your statement, please, where you say this:

'My complaint to General Brims ... (about hooding and
stress positions) caused considerable disquiet.'
How were you made aware of that?

MERCER: It was just obvious. It was not popular.

ELIAS: Say that again.

MERCER: It was just obvious. It was not very popular.
I understand subsequently that the commandant of the
prisoner of war camp had also seen it and raised his
concerns and, of course, whilst I was being told I was
wrong, at this point the Red Cross picked up on it and it
was now – obviously once the Red Cross had got on it, it
was a turbo-charged issue.

ELIAS: At those meetings where the ICRC [Red Cross] were
raising concerns about hooding, was there any attempt to
justify the use of hooding for any purpose by any of the
British representatives?

MERCER: Yes.

ELIAS: What was your attitude to that when it was raised, that
security was a reason for hooding?

MERCER: Well, I was – I didn't accept it for a minute. I
thought there was no requirement at all and I thought
it was not the way that hooding was actually being used
when I'd seen it.

ELIAS: So it would be fair, would it, to say that you didn't
believe that is why it was being used –

MERCER: I was hard over hooding. I just find the whole
thing repulsive. In my view it amounts to violence and
intimidation and it degrades the individual. So I don't like
it at all under any circumstances.

ELIAS: And you made that clear at the meeting, did you?

MERCER: I was instructed not to speak at the meeting.

ELIAS: I want to ask you about that, of course. You were
instructed not to speak about what?

MERCER: About anything.

ELIAS: And by whom were you so instructed?

MERCER: I think it's probably on the list of ciphers.

ELIAS: Did you walk out of any meeting at which the Red Cross were present?

MERCER: I did walk out at one point, yes.

ELIAS: Why did you walk out?

MERCER: Because I was very cross with some of the excuses that were being put forward, what I saw as excuses.

ELIAS: What, excuses for hooding?

MERCER: Yes.

ELIAS: Colonel Mercer, in the course of what I am going to categorise as general discussions about this issue of hooding and whether it was justified in any way, was the shock of capture referred to by anyone as any sort of justification to your recollection?

MERCER: I didn't understand it in the sense that you put a hood over someone's head – I mean, the shock is there because you have been captured.

ELIAS: I just want to ask you this about it: that was your assumption, was it, that the matter would go, as it were, all the way up to ministers?

MERCER: I am not sure how much I am allowed to say. But, yes, I think if the Red Cross is going to make an official complaint to a government, which is what it does, then there is no way that this thing would have stayed at the level of [senior military commanders on the ground]. It would have gone all the way up.

ELIAS: That's what you assumed would happen?

MERCER: I did, yes.

ELIAS: Moving on now to 20 May – [four months before Baha Mousa's death] you were advised by the [military police] that there had been a death in custody of someone held by a battlegroup and that that matter was being investigated.

MERCER: That's correct.

ELIAS: You were also led to believe that there may have been other deaths in British custody. Having been alerted to two deaths, what then did you do about it?

MERCER: Well, it wasn't just two deaths. There were a number of deaths – I thought the figure was higher.

ELIAS: Can I take you, please, to paragraph 99 of your statement, under the heading 'Conclusion', in which you say: 'There was a general indifference to prisoners which was reflected, initially, in the lack of manpower and resources provided.'
Again do you mean indifference brought about by a lack of resources or indifference demonstrated in other ways?

MERCER: I think by this stage this went wider. I think actually the lack of resources reflected a general lack of consideration for what was going to be a massive issue and indeed it was.

ELIAS: You reflect that, don't you, in paragraph 100, where you say: 'I am still amazed that we had to fight so hard for even basic Geneva Convention rights for prisoners.'

MERCER: That's correct.

ELIAS: You say: 'This indifference ... was exacerbated by the total strategic failure to plan for Occupation and the vacuum it created.'

MERCER: Yes.

ELIAS: Then this at paragraph 101: 'In my view, if the issue of prisoners had been properly resourced and we had been allowed to implement a proper reviewing and oversight mechanism then the tragedy which unfolded might never have happened.'

MERCER: Yes, I agree with that.

ELIAS: By the 'tragedy', are you referring to the particular matter that this Inquiry is investigating?

MERCER: Yes, I am here. I think if we had had a proper reviewing process in place, I think if we had had a judge in theatre, as we requested, with a detainee/internee management unit, if we had had an independent team for prisoners and I think if there wasn't this constant reluctance to accept high legal standards, then I think we could have avoided this tragedy.

ELIAS: You go on in the final two lines of your statement to say: 'Ultimately, however, given the vagaries of all warfare, in my view, it's also about proper education, training and the moral compass.'

MERCER: Yes.

ELIAS: Proper education, training and the moral compass for whom?

MERCER: This is the wider point. I mean, all staff officers deal with problems within a military operation, but let's face it whenever this is going on then every time a soldier abuses a prisoner, there is generally a junior NCO present who should know what to do, there is generally a senior NCO present who knows what to do. There is generally a Platoon Commander, there is generally a Company Commander overseeing that Unit. You cannot stop those sort of things simply by staff work. It is impossible. It pops up somewhere else. It's what happens on the ground and if soldiers are taught to intervene rather than turn a blind eye – and this is what I refer to as the moral compass.

ADAM INGRAM 2 JUNE 2010:
ADAM PATERSON INGRAM (affirmed)

CHAIRMAN: If I could ask you, please, to keep as close as you reasonably can – I think it is not all that comfortable – you have a fairly loud voice, if I may say so, so I am sure we will have no trouble in hearing you.

ELIAS: [In] June 2001, you were appointed Minister of State at the Ministry of Defence, responsible for the armed forces.

INGRAM: I was, yes.

ELIAS: And that was a post that you held, you tell us, until June 2007?

INGRAM: That's correct.

ELIAS: It follows that you were in that office in the spring of 2004, when abuse allegations, particularly relating to Iraq, surfaced in the media.

INGRAM: I was, yes. I was responsible across a range of issues. It was a very busy post.

ELIAS: Did you have any knowledge, at the time of planning for Iraq, as to whether it was or was not proper or appropriate for soldiers to hood or deprive of sight prisoners that they may take?

INGRAM: No, I wouldn't have any more than I would have had a close intimate knowledge of other operational requirements placed upon military personnel such as rules of engagement.

ELIAS: Are you telling the Inquiry, to the best of your recollection, that the issue of hooding was something that was never discussed with you prior to deployment to Iraq?

INGRAM: I would – that would be accurate, yes.

ELIAS: I am going to ask you this question or something like it perhaps a number of times. Let me ask you for the first time now: your position in taking on the responsibilities that you [had] as Minister of State, meant, of course, that you had responsibility for these areas, but you also had, didn't you, a duty, as it were, to be answerable to Parliament and through them to the public –

INGRAM: That is correct, yes.

ELIAS: So it might be said that you did need to know about certain matters where it was likely to be a matter that became public through the media or otherwise so that you could deal with it and answer questions, either [in] Parliament or outside Parliament, appropriately, fully and accurately.

INGRAM: Well, I would have been dependent upon the advice being forwarded to me through the Department and I would have to be dependent upon the quality of that advice as being accurate and honest.

ELIAS: It didn't occur to you that the armed forces would be acting in any way unlawfully.

INGRAM: Absolutely. I mean I would take the view that all military planning would have been done in full conformity with both domestic and international law. We would have expected all forces, to be sensitive to the needs of the local population: don't make enemies, make friends.

ELIAS: Does it mean that you would have regarded your involvement in these areas as only arising if and when something went wrong?

INGRAM: No, I think it would have been a case of mutual respect between ministers and those in the hot position in the front-line, and there had to be honesty at all levels in that.

ELIAS: You used the phrase 'honesty at all levels'. I just want to understand what you meant by that.

INGRAM: Well, it would be that. There would have to be people telling you – the phrase that would have been used would have been people telling you ground truth. There was no point trying to obscure or dissemble or to deny reality.

ELIAS: I think you will know that the Inquiry has been made aware that the ICRC [International Committee of the Red Cross] made a complaint or raised issues in relation to the handling of prisoners – hoods, being left out in the sun, the possibility at least of stress positions being used by our forces – in late March or thereabouts 2003. Did you know about that complaint at the time?

INGRAM: I have no recollection of being aware of it at the time.

ELIAS: You are likely to have a recollection, if indeed you were told, of ICRC [a Red Cross] complaint about hooding prisoners at a relatively early stage, are you not?

INGRAM: Well, I think my political antennae would have been alert enough in that sense to have been made aware that I was being told something that I should be aware of it, and if it was a request for action on my part, then I would have addressed that.

ELIAS: If we have a look, please, at MOD050331. You will be very familiar with these letters, Mr Ingram, where you are responding to an MP no doubt raising a matter on behalf of a constituent.

INGRAM: Yes, I am aware of that, yes.

ELIAS: This is May 2003. If we look at the last paragraph of this letter, going out in your name to Michael Foster MP, you say this at the third line: 'There were a small number of occasions at the start of the conflict where prisoners were hooded for short periods – this practice has now been stopped.' That's information that you would have accepted in a draft before you signed this letter, is it?

INGRAM: It wasn't just a case of being given a draft letter and signing it off. There would be a full explanation as to the content of that letter coming from those who had responsibility to properly report to me on this.

ELIAS: But the letter would also have been drafted for you, would it?

INGRAM: That's correct, yes.

ELIAS: If we read on in that last paragraph, please: 'But I would like to reassure your constituent that in all this we have worked very closely with the ICRC [Red Cross] who have expressed themselves content with the way we have treated prisoners and detainees throughout the conflict.' Had you known that the ICRC [Red Cross] had raised a complaint in March/April [2003], corroborated indeed by soldiers who have given evidence to this Inquiry, that prisoners were hooded, left out in the sun, [in] stress positions, could you have said that in this letter?

INGRAM: It would have depended upon the nature of what the originating complaint was. Of course, these letters were probably being generated by anti-war groups, by Amnesty International and by a range of other organisations.

ELIAS: Well, that's as may be, but it is the fact, isn't it, that if it is right that there was a complaint by ICRC [the Red Cross] and if it is right that prisoners were hooded, were left out in sun for hours, hooded, put in stress positions, it would not have been entirely accurate – forget the honesty bit – to say, 'The ICRC [Red Cross] have expressed themselves content with the way we have treated the prisoners and detainees throughout the conflict'. That simply would not have been accurate, would it?

INGRAM: I don't know whether it referred to the specific complaint that you have noted and whether that would have been brought to my attention, whether I would have had a knowledge of that. I need to see the background note. I would then need to judge why I would not have included that in the draft letter that had been presented to me.

ELIAS: Accepting the fact of a complaint, this letter, putting it neutrally, would not appear to have been telling accurately the ICRC [Red Cross] position and the British Government's position throughout the conflict, would it?

INGRAM: Well, I would need to see just what the ICRC [Red Cross] complaint was I have no recollection of being aware of it.

ELIAS: May I just ask this one last time and I shall then move on. The last two lines of the letter: 'The ICRC [Red Cross], who have expressed themselves content with the way we have treated prisoners and detainees throughout the conflict ...'
Would you have put your signature to that if you had known that, a month or so earlier, there had been a complaint made by the ICRC [Red Cross] which, in fact, complained that prisoners were hooded, left in the sun and possibly left in stress positions? Would you have put your signature to the letter as it is there drafted?

INGRAM: I would have probably tried to establish ground truth.
There was nothing to be gained from people telling something that wasn't true because the truth would always surface. So I don't think it was a denial of honesty. I think it was dealing with the ground truth at that point in time and correcting any feelings that may have arisen.

ELIAS: That doesn't quite address my question, Mr Ingram, which is really this: we know what you did write, we know what you signed because it is there in black and white.

Looking back even with hindsight, if you like, do you think now, given that you were going to be writing letters of that kind, it would have been better had you been told in March or April 2003 that the ICRC [Red Cross] have made a serious complaint about the way prisoners are being handled?

INGRAM: Without seeing the nature of what the ICRC [Red Cross] has said, I don't know whether it was serious or not.

ELIAS: Then I will move on. You tell us in your statement that you didn't see the Sky News footage, I think broadcast in April 2003, of Iraqi detainees hooded.

INGRAM: Yes. I do not recall seeing the footage. You know, I do not recall that, but it's – I may not have been in the country.

ELIAS: Again, if you had seen that, would it not have shocked you?

INGRAM: I think it would have done, yes.

ELIAS: If you had seen it, wouldn't it have been something that caused you to make some inquiry?

INGRAM: There's no evidence that I didn't make an inquiry.

ELIAS: If you didn't see it, which is your recollection, do you not find it astonishing that the fact that there was such footage was not brought to your attention, [as] the minister?

INGRAM: Well it may have been, but I don't recollect that being – I go back to my earlier comments. I was involved in that whole range of different issues.

ELIAS: Can I move on, then, please? Still looking at your state of knowledge, if you like, Baha Mousa's death, do you recall being told of his death?

INGRAM: I remember seeing – I have seen the briefing note that came up that referred to two incidents. One was his death; another one was the injury to a child.

ELIAS: You say in your statement to this Inquiry that when you heard of the death of Baha Mousa, as I understand it, you recall being shocked.

INGRAM: Yes, I do, yes.

ELIAS: What was it that shocked you, do you remember?

INGRAM: Well there were two elements to that. One was the injury to the child and the death of someone in detention. It is not something which should have happened.

ELIAS: Can we have a look at [what] would appear to be a briefing note to the Secretary of State, copied to you and your private secretary, MOD048699.

In paragraph 5, the detail that you were given in this document:

'Although the individual did not need to be forcibly restrained on arrest, advice from theatre suggests that he consistently struggled with his cuffs and hood during the day, repeatedly tried to escape and also allegedly lashed out at guards. At 18.40 Iraqi time the individual slipped his hood. Two members of the guard restrained him and replaced his hood. His pulse was also apparently checked at this time. Three minutes later the guard suspected that he might not be breathing.'

Pausing there, that, therefore, was telling you, wasn't it, that a detainee had been hooded perhaps within minutes of his collapsing and subsequently dying?

INGRAM: That's correct.

ELIAS: It goes on: 'The detainee was declared dead at 1905 hours.' Then you are given this additional information: 'At this point the individual had been in custody for a total of 36 hours. He had spent 23 hours and 40 minutes of this hooded, albeit not continually. We are continuing to investigate the circumstances surrounding the incident and will provide further information when we have it.'

If we look, please, at document MOD048704 dated 18 September, a similar updated briefing note; correct?

INGRAM: Yes.

ELIAS: You can see in the top right-hand corner a handwritten [note] says this, doesn't it? 'This could be very messy. 2 soldiers have been arrested. Minister (AF) ...' That would be you.

INGRAM: Yes, that's correct.

ELIAS: '... will deal as lead minister.'

INGRAM: Correct, yes.

ELIAS: Were you horrified to learn that prisoners were being kept hooded for 24 hours in 36?

INGRAM: Horrified? Strong word. It does say albeit not continually. I wouldn't have put a value judgement on it until I had established best information and ground truth on this.

ELIAS: When these matters were raised with you, did you stop then to think [to] yourself, 'Well, is this humane? Is it lawful? Is it a matter about which I need legal advice?'

INGRAM: I probably received that.

ELIAS: Was the fact that maybe there was something, as some witnesses had put it, thin about the written doctrine – inadequate about the written doctrine, if you like – was that fact or the fact that perhaps the training of forces in this area needed to be looked at, was that ever brought to your attention?

INGRAM: I have no recollection of that being brought to my attention. What I am saying is I have no recollection, but that's not to say that it wasn't brought to my attention.

ELIAS: I understand. What's the answer to my question?

INGRAM: They should have been.

ELIAS: Should it have been brought to your attention?

INGRAM: The answer to that is 'yes'.

ELIAS: Of course, you had responsibility not only for the Iraq conflict, but for the conduct of soldiers wherever they were deployed throughout the world, didn't you?

INGRAM: Correct.

ELIAS: Did you not consider, when these issues of hooding were being raised in this specific theatre, that what was needed was a clear direction, a clear legal view, if you like?

INGRAM: But there was a debate about the legal view and my recollection tells me that a similar discussion was taking place in relation to Afghanistan and the handling of detainees, insurgents or whatever else, and how we should deal with them, whether we should turn them over –

ELIAS: Wasn't this something that cried out for direction from the top?

INGRAM: There was no evidence that there was no direction from the top.

ELIAS: Did you give any on the use of hoods?

INGRAM: Did I give any on the – well, I don't have the paperwork to prove or disprove that that did or did not happen, but let me assure you that there was intensive discussion going on about the use of hoods and its appropriateness because there were differing legal approaches in all of this.

ELIAS: I don't misrepresent you, do I, if I say that your evidence is, then, that you have no recollection of taking any proactive step to ascertain a clear line for hooding to be cascaded down from the Ministry?

INGRAM: I don't accept that there was an omission on my part. I do not have the paperwork, I do not have the paper trail, to show whether it was proactive or not.

ELIAS: Now we have the extract from Hansard [MOD050379], what you actually said [on the 28th] June 2004; do you see? If we go into the right-hand column after the second half under 'Interrogation techniques', as a heading.

INGRAM: I have that, yes.

ELIAS: 'Mr McNamara: To ask the Secretary of State for Defence when he was first informed that UK forces in Iraq were practising the banned interrogation technique of hooding prisoners; if he will list the regiments in which the practice was identified; and on what date and on whose authority an order was issued to cease the practice.'

Your answer, [on the 28th] June 2004: 'We are not aware of any incidents in which United Kingdom interrogators are alleged to have used hooding as an interrogation technique.'

INGRAM: I see that yes.

ELIAS: We have also seen, haven't we, the briefing to the Secretary of State copied to you – which you would have read, you tell us – which said in terms that a prisoner had been hooded.

INGRAM: I would need to go back to see that. I need to see the precise term of that background note.

ELIAS: That might have affected the way that you answered the question, might it? Might it have affected the way that you answered the question?

INGRAM: It may have done or may not have done, but since it is something that has been brought to my attention, I think I would need to see precisely what was said in that background note.

ELIAS: Can we go back then, please? This is what you were being told in September 2003 MOD048704: 'In this instance the tactical questioning of the suspects was conducted by two Intelligence Corps Staff Sergeants, both fully trained in [tactical questioning]. It would appear that the hooding of the suspects took place on the advice of one of the staff sergeants.'
Do you need more?

INGRAM: No, I think – yes.

ELIAS: So if we go back to your answer [in The House of Commons], please – appreciating time has moved on – if you had had that in mind, Mr Ingram, would you have answered that question [on the 28th] June 2004 as you in fact did answer it?

INGRAM: It certainly wouldn't have been within my power to have remembered everything that I had been informed in writing or verbally. I would have been wholly dependent upon best advice from the Department on this.

CHAIRMAN: Mr Ingram, if we look at the date, 18 September 2003 – a reference there to tactical questioners, saying that a suspect was hooded, and it refers to the Baha Mousa incident, does it not?

INGRAM: It does, yes.

CHAIRMAN: It would appear to indicate that the tactical questioners had asked for Mr Baha Mousa to be hooded for the purposes of interrogation.
That would seem to be a fair reading of that?

INGRAM: With respect, Sir, I don't necessarily read it that way.

CHAIRMAN: Now if I could ask you just, please, to look at something again. You were asked about your answer [on the 28th June 2004] to a parliamentary question by Mr McNamara.
The background note we have is MOD050381, if you could put that up on the screen. What [your military assistant] really appears to be pointing out to you is that the question asks about interrogation and you do not need to answer about using hooding for security purposes.

INGRAM: Correct, yes. He is more or less saying don't elaborate –

CHAIRMAN: Because otherwise you may get into problems over hooding in transit or you may have to speak about that; is that right?

INGRAM: I don't think into problems –

CHAIRMAN: I say 'problems'. You may have to explain.

INGRAM: Why impart information that is not being sought would be the approach.